FOLKESTONE
PAST AND PRESENT

FOLKESTONE
PAST AND PRESENT

ALAN F. TAYLOR

Published in association with

First published in Great Britain by The Breedon Books Publishing Company Limited
Breedon House, 44 Friar Gate, Derby, DE1 1DA. 1999

This paperback edition published in Great Britain in 2015 by DB Publishing, an imprint of JMD Media Ltd

© Alan E. Taylor, 2002

All Rights Reserved. No part of this publication may be reproduced, stored in a retrieval system, or transmitted in any form, or by any means, electronic, mechanical, photocopying, recording or otherwise without the prior permission in writing of the copyright holders, nor be otherwise circulated in any form or binding or cover other than in which it is published and without a similar condition being imposed on the subsequent publisher.

ISBN 978-1-78091-492-3

Printed and bound in the UK by Copytech (UK) Ltd Peterborough

Contents

Acknowledgements 6

Introduction 7

Chronology of the Recent History of the Town 9

The Leas 12

Lower Sandgate Road and Sea Front 22

The Harbour 32

East Cliff and Warren 45

Places of Entertainment 58

Churches and Chapels 66

Hotels and Public Houses 72

Streets and Trades 89

Bibliography 160

Acknowledgements

I would like to extend my sincere thanks to the following people and organisations for the assistance they gave me while I was compiling this publication. Without them, it would have been much the poorer.

My dear wife Eileen for the lack of attention that I have paid her during the past three months of writing.

My son Andrew for writing the introduction, and for all his support, advice, and proof reading.

The staff of the Heritage Room, Folkestone Library, for all their help.

Adrian Harrison from Seymour Harrison photographers, for all his help and advice.

Peter and Anne Bamford, Eamonn Rooney, Dennis Pullen, Mrs G. Hoad, and P.J. Davies for allowing me to copy photographs from their collections.

Introduction

IN THIS photographic history of Folkestone past and present, we are invited to observe the development of the town over a period starting in the 1850s and continuing up until the present day. It is roughly within this time span that Folkestone developed from being a small fishing town, considerably behind in its development when compared to other coastal towns in Kent and Sussex, into being a thriving and fashionable seaside resort, complete with a railway connection to London and a cross-Channel port.

Excavations have shown that the region of Folkestone has been populated from prehistoric times and the existence of a villa on the East Cliff dating from the Roman period, which was discovered in 1924, shows us that Folkestone has been inhabited for over two millennia. The Saxons and the Jutes were also present in the area as burial grounds bear testimony and we know that in AD c.635 Eanswythe, daughter of Eadbald King of Kent, founded a religious house in the locale of the Bayle. And in accordance with the miracles attributed to her, Eanswythe was canonised. To this day the Parish Church is dedicated to Saints Mary and Eanswythe. The first church bearing her name was destroyed following cliff erosion; the second was destroyed c.867 by Viking raiders. Another church, built by King Athelstan, was presumed to have been destroyed in 1052 by Earl Godwin on the way to his showdown with King Edward the Confessor. In 1095 Nigel de Muneville succeeded as lord of the manor and to him is attributed the basis of the modern day Parish Church.

One important statistic can be gleaned from the Domesday survey, which tells us that the Folkestone 'Hundred' was valued at £100, and we can estimate that at this time there was a population of about 800 people.

In 1313 Folkestone received a Charter from King Edward II, which entitled it to a mayor, a bailiff and 12 jurats. By this time Folkestone had become a member of the confederation of Cinque Ports, but the small market town and port of Folkestone was not destined to grow significantly, Tudor Folkestone had a population of approximately 500 people.

Bearing this in mind, it should be of little surprise that by 1831 the population of Folkestone had grown to only 3,638. This is an interesting fact because in the intervening period there had been a nationwide shift of the population out of rural England and into urban centres, brought about by factors such as the Industrial Revolution. Statistics show that in approximately 300 years the population had grown only sevenfold. Compare this to later population statistics and we can see how small Folkestone's growth and development was over this period of time.

However, times and circumstances were to change. In 1843 the railway came from London and the viaduct crossing the Foord valley was built. This was followed by the purchase of the harbour by the South-Eastern Railway that succeeded in transforming the ailing harbour into a successful cross-Channel port. The significance of these events can be best registered when we note that by 1851 the population had nearly doubled from 20 years previous to 6,726 people. By 1881 this trend continued and the population soared to 18,986 people; within a period of 50 years the town's population had grown by a staggering 522 per cent. It was an enormous rate of growth when compared to the earlier statistics that cover hundreds of years.

The arrival of the railway and the development of the harbour instantly expanded the possibilities that Folkestone had to offer. Large and luxurious hotels were built along with many other amenities that were needed to cater for the holiday-making public.

World War One was to change the shape of Folkestone however, with large numbers of refugees arriving and the use of the harbour as a prime military embarkation point, the town rapidly adjusted. In between the wars, Folkestone once again rejuvenated itself and became a resort that would appeal to middle-class families and not just the affluent upper classes.

Following World War Two and the damage

caused by 77 air-raids and six V1 attacks, Folkestone yet again had to rebuild and re-design itself in order to continue in its function as a resort for holiday-makers and day-trippers. Much has happened to the town in the period since 1945; extensive rebuilding programmes and the expansion of residential and light-industrial areas, the building of the M20 and the Channel Tunnel, has all meant that Folkestone has undergone several changes.

This, therefore, is the aim and purpose of this book, to show the reader just how much the town has grown, developed and changed over the years. The use of photographic comparison, showing locations and buildings in their past and present incarnations, speaks volumes more about the town's rapid development than would a book that sought simply to describe its evolution in words alone.

The use of photographs enables the reader to conjure up graphic images of times, places and ways of life that have long since gone. The photographs from the past show us not only how buildings and areas have changed, or in some cases disappeared, but also how fashion has developed, how society has changed, how modes of transport and the frequency of their use has altered.

One wonders how, in 50 years time someone may take a look at this book and comment and reflect upon how much the town has changed since 2002; in much the same way as we looking at this same publication marvel at the changes so evident from the comparisons we are shown.

Will future generations learn from the mistakes made by so many 20th-century planners and developers who have sometimes changed the face of this town for the worst – who knows?

But what we can be certain of is that through books such as this one, we can chart the progress of a town's development for the better and for the worse, not only for our own reference but also for those of a future generation.

Andrew Taylor
Folkestone
Summer 2002

Chronology of the Recent History of the Town

1805-6   Martello Towers erected for defence of the coast.

1807   Act of Parliament for constructing a pier and harbour. Folkestone Harbour Company was formed.

1808   Foundation stone of Folkestone Harbour Pier was laid.

1814   Folkestone Union Charity School – British and Foreign Schools Society – founded in the Apollo Room. In 1835 the school was moved to the former Folkestone Workhouse, then on the site of Dover Road School. The present Dover Road School (corner of St John's Street) was opened 1887. Re-named Hillside in 1951 New Hillside Secondary School for boys opened at Park Farm in 1958.

1825   Act of Parliament enabling Lord Radnor to grant lease for the building of the Folkestone estate.

1828   Lord Radnor constructs Lower Sandgate Road.

1830   Cistern House adopted as Town Hall. Built by Lord Radnor and hired to Corporation. Demolished 1858.

1842   First Gas Works established on the beach.

1843   South-Eastern Railway Company bought the harbour for £18,000.

1843   Railway line from London opened.

1843   First Channel Packet operated from 1 August. First boat was the *William Wallace*.

1843   Harbour House with Clock Tower was built.

1843   The Pavilion Hotel was started. (Hotel enlarged in 1845 and 1850.)

1846   The Dispensary founded in Rendezvous Street.

1848   Building of Guildhall Street begun.

1849   Branch line to harbour, swing bridge and terminal station built.

1850   Christ Church built.

1852   Opening of the New National School in Cheriton Road. Christ Church School.

1854   St Mary's National School built in Dover Road; opened 1855.

1855   Queen Victoria visited Shorncliffe Camp.

1855   Charles Dickens stayed for three months at No.3 Albion Villas.

1856   Congregational Church built in Tontine Street.

1857   West Cliff Hotel (Majestic) opened 22 August.

1857   Cheriton Road Cemetery opened.

1859   Bates Hotel opened (Esplanade).

1860   Marine Terrace commenced building.

1861   New Town Hall opened.

1861   Promenade Pier begun.

1862   Bouverie Square building commenced 8 February.

1862   St Peters Church built on East Cliff (enlarged 1870).

1863   Homesdale Terrace commenced building.

1863   New houses built on the Leas (Royal Terrace).

1865   Clifton Gardens East was built.

1865   St Michael's Church opened; first built in wood.

1865   Wesleyan Methodist Church building commenced.

1866   Old Gas Works on beach demolished. Works moved to Foord Road.

1866   Improvements to Rendezvous Street adopted.

1868   Holy Trinity Church opened.

1869   Bathing Establishment (Marina) opened.

1871   Wesleyan School opened under Chapel (closed 1926).

1872   St Peters School opened.

1874   Radnor Club opened 30 May.

1874   Folkestone Rowing Club formation 15 May (the clubhouse was built in 1884).

1877   Formation of The New Shorncliffe Road.

1877   Clifton Gardens West was built.

FOLKESTONE: PAST AND PRESENT

1878 Bradstone Hall was built.
1879 Public Library opened on the Bayle.
1879 St John's Church, consecration began 11am on Monday 3 February.
1881 Harvey Statue unveiled.
1882 Wesleyan Chapel and School in the Canterbury road opened.
1882 St Saviour's Church – Lord Radnor's gift of a site for, and the opening of a temporary Iron Church.
1882 The Salvation Army Barracks – Purchase of Bradstone Hall.
1884 Central Station built. First named Cheriton Arch; renamed Radnor Park in 1886, and finally renamed Central Station in 1895.
1884 Opening of St Andrew's Convalescent Home.
1885 Leas Lift opened, 16 September.
1885 Mundella School opened – formally North Council School.
1885 Queen's Hotel opened.
1885 Opening of Pavilion Winter Gardens 21 March.
1885 The Osborne Temperance Hotel opened by Lord Folkestone.
1885 Grace Hill Improvements – The first plot of ground purchased by the Freemasons for £500 for a Masonic Hall.
1886 Art Treasures Exhibition opened in Bouverie Road West.
1886 Wampach Hotel opened.
1886 Radnor Park opened.
1888 Victoria Pier opened 21 July.
1888 Switchback Railway was built.
1888 Pleasure Gardens Theatre opened.
1888 New Library and Museum opened on Grace Hill.
1889 St John the Baptist's Church opened in Foord.
1890 3 July Victoria Hospital was officially opened by HRH Alfred Duke of Edinburgh.
1893 Folkestone Amusements Association formed.
1893 Lower Sandgate Road was laid out.
1893 Marine Gardens Bandstand was built.
1893 Sandgate Hill Lift opened. Closed 1918.
1893 Lifeboat House erected, Lower Sandgate Road.
1894 Leas Shelter opened.
1895 Lower Leas Bandstand erected.
1896 Technical School opened.
1897 Metropole Hotel opened on 1 July.
1897 Sydney Street School opened.
1898 Electricity Works started.
1901 First motor omnibus service started between Folkestone and Hythe.
1902 Leas Pavilion opened.
1902 West Leas Bandstand rebuilt; transferred from the Metropole Hotel gardens.
1902 Hill Road constructed by Lord Radnor.
1903 Grand Hotel opened as the Grand Mansions on 12 September.
1904 West Leas Lift (Metropole) opened 31 March and closed 1939.
1905 Cricket Ground opened (Cheriton Road).
1905 Folkestone County School for Girls founded.
1910 Electric Theatre (Savoy) opened.
1910 First part of Marine Promenade was built.
1912 Queen's Cinema, Tontine Street opened.
1912 Playhouse Cinema opened in Guildhall Street.
1912 Central Cinema opened in George Lane.
1913 Leas and West Cliff Walks leased to Folkestone Corporation.
1915 Belgian refugees crowd into the town.
1917 Air Raid on town 25 May caused heavy casualties 71 killed and 96 injured.
1921 Zig-Zag Path constructed on the Leas.
1924 Roman Villas excavated on the East Cliff.
1926 Marine Gardens Pavilion completed.
1927 Leas Cliff Hall opened by Prince Henry.
1928 Kingsnorth Gardens opened on site of clay pit.
1929 Arthur Brough's, first season at the Leas Pavilion. Arthur Brough was later famous in *Are You Being Served*.
1931 Bobby's Store transferred from Rendezvous Street to new premises in Sandgate Road.
1934 East Cliff Pavilion opened.
1935 Astoria Cinema opened 20 April (renamed Odeon Cinema in 1940).

CHRONOLOGY OF THE RECENT HISTORY OF THE TOWN

1935	Coronation Parade on the East Cliff Sands was opened.
1935	House demolished in the Fishmarket due to a landslip.
1936	Open-air swimming pool on the beach opened 11 July.
1937	Rotunda amusement park opened.
1939	Many Folkestone schoolchildren evacuated to Wales. Resident population reduced to 12,000.
1945	Victoria Pier destroyed by fire on Whit Monday.
1955	New bus station opened in Bouverie Square.
1958	Marina (bathing establishment) closed.
1958	Visit of Queen and Prince Philip.
1959	The Metropole Hotel closed and was converted into luxury flats.
1960	Sunny Sands restaurant opened at the Stade.
1962	Central Station rebuilt and line electrified.
1962	Majestic Hotel, formerly West Cliff, closed.
1962	Queen's Hotel closed.
1967	New Civic Centre opened in Castle Hill Avenue.
1970	Trinity House Pilot Station erected.
1972	Car Ferry Terminal opened at Folkestone Harbour.
1972	Building of the Northern Distributor Road commenced.
1973	The Grand Hotel closed and was converted into luxury flats.
1984	The official opening of the new shopping precinct, building started on 29 May.
2000	Official opening of the first phase of the Lower Leas Coastal Park, Saturday 27 May.

The Leas

MONSIEUR de Bouverie, Earle of Radnor, purchased the Leas area and other tracts of land in Folkestone in 1697. At the time the Leas was open farmland. In 1825 Lord Radnor secured an Act of Parliament to enable building leases to be granted of part of the settled estates of Jacob, Earl of Radnor in the parishes of Folkestone and Cheriton, and he made available to local builders, plots of land on long leases to stimulate building enterprise. But progress was extremely slow and nothing substantial seems to have been done for 20 years. So Lord Radnor appointed a London architect, Mr Sydney Smirke, to develop the estate. One of his plans was for the development of the West Cliff. However, Lord Radnor did not begin development until 1845; the upper Leas Gardens were laid out parallel to the development and progressed westwards. The laying out of the Upper Leas promenade and the building of elegant villas, boarding houses, hotels, concert halls, and three cliff lifts followed this – the Sandgate Lift, Metropole Lift and the Leas Lift. Two bandstands were constructed, the Upper Leas Bandstand in 1897 and the West Leas Bandstand originally located behind the Metropole Hotel was relocated to its new position on the Leas in 1902, however, it, was subsequently demolished in 1948.

The Leas is a Kentish dialect word meaning 'a common, or open space of pasture'.

By the middle of the 19th century Folkestone had become a fashionable resort frequented by royalty and the aristocracy.

The church parade was a great feature being a very fashionable gathering; the spectacle on a Sunday morning in the season was one not to be forgotten. The Leas, from end to end, was crowded with ladies and gentlemen dressed in the latest fashions; the effect was one of brilliancy and colour, caused by the stream of people, and groups of friends chatting together as they occupied the chairs which were liberally dotted about for the purpose.

In 1913 the Leas Cliff, from West Terrace to Metropole Road West was leased to the Corporation for 999 years at an annual rent of £1. The Zig-Zag path was constructed with Pulhamite Rock in 1921, the path is of an easy gradient without steps to the Under Cliff, Riviera Drive, Marine Parade, Marine Gardens, and the beach and bathing.

In 1934 the Corporation leased another section of the park from Lord Radnor's estate from Metropole Road West to Martello Tower number four.

The Sandgate Lift closed in 1918, the Metropole Lift closed during World War Two.

After World War Two, Folkestone saw a substantial decline in the holiday trade so it began to cater for day-trippers, language students and short-break visitors. Quite a number of hotels and boarding houses on the Leas were demolished and replaced with modern blocks of flats, and in 1966 one of the two Leas Lifts closed.

However, the Leas today remains a very fine walk along the cliff top with superb sea views, fine lawns and well-kept flowerbeds.

The east end of the Leas on a bright sunny day in the early 1880s. In Victorian times people dressed to keep the sun off them, as illustrated here by the ladies with their parasols up. The photograph was taken just before the Leas Lift was built. Between the first two buildings on the left (second one being the Longford Hotel) is where the Leas Club now stands.

The present-day east end of the Leas on a sunny day in October 2001; the Victorian buildings were demolished in c.1969 to make way for these modern blocks of flats. The local builder Jenner & Sons Ltd built the tall building, formerly Fortune House, in 1969-70, for the Welfare Insurance Company, at a cost of £700,000. The building is 127ft high and it has 36,710 square feet of floor space on seven floors. The Welfare Insurance Company moved to Devon in June 1978 and the building remained empty until 1987 when it was converted into flats.

The East End of the Leas: looking west in the late 1920s. The Leas Pavilion can be seen on the extreme right of the picture, the sign over the entrance is advertising variety shows, 4pm and 8pm, while in the centre Mr Hayes is giving Punch and Judy shows.

The East End of the Leas: looking west in October 2001. On the right can be seen the Leas Club formerly the Leas Pavilion. The Victorian buildings seen in the last picture have been demolished and replaced with this complex of 38 flats and 18 maisonettes with underground parking, which was completed in November 1971.

The Leas: looking west in the 1920s, the Lower Leas Bandstand and the Salisbury Hotel dominate the picture. The Lower Leas Bandstand was erected opposite Clifton Gardens in 1895. During the summer season bands played daily, and fashionable crowds sat on chairs around the bandstand to listen to A. Newmann's Red Hungarian Band or Herr Worm's Blue Viennese Band.

The Leas Bandstand and Salisbury Hotel in October 2001. This bandstand is the only one out of three to survive. Note the building behind the Bandstand; it is at the end of Clifton Crescent. Long gone are the days when Lord Radnor's policemen patrolled the Leas to remove any undesirables.

The Zig-Zag Path and the Leas. After World War One the number of unemployed men grew rapidly. The Corporation decided to construct the Zig-Zag path with Pulhamite Rock designed by Mr J.R. Pulham from Margate with the aid of some of these unemployed men. The path is an easy gradient without steps to the Under Cliff, Riviera Drive, Marine Parade, Marine Gardens, the beach and bathing.

The Zig-Zag path as it looks now, rather more overgrown than in the earlier picture. In 1971 there was an earth slip and part of the path collapsed. To repair it a flight of steps were added, thus defeating the original object of a path that could be used for perambulators and the disabled. The steps have now been removed and the path is back to how it was originally built.

The Leas and Lower Leas Bandstand: looking east. There is a band playing in the bandstand and the Leas is thronging with people taking their daily stroll, some with their perambulators and some taking rides in bath chairs. The Leas was the place for elegant ladies to be seen promenading before and after church parade. It was the place for mothers to show off their eligible daughters.

The Leas and Lower Leas Bandstand in October 2001. Note the lack of people, unfortunately it is a sign of the times, the younger generation need to ride everywhere in their cars. Note the bollards in the middle of the path, they denote the access to the Zig-Zag path, and are a new addition. On the extreme left can be seen a windbreak for people listening to the band, it is an extremely useful addition.

The Leas and Metropole Bandstand: looking east. This bandstand was originally erected in the grounds of the hotel, between the hotel wings, for their guests. Unfortunately the sounds reverberated from the walls and disturbed them. So the proprietors of the hotel gave the bandstand to the Corporation, who erected it on the West Leas in front of the hotel in 1902.

The West End of the Leas: looking east. It's interesting to note the lack of people promenading along the Leas and that the bandstand has now gone. It was demolished by the Corporation and sold for scrap in 1948. The modern block of flats seen in the distance is at the end of Clifton Crescent, the Victorian building was demolished and these flats were built on the site in about 1964.

The Leas looking west: showing the Upper Leas Bandstand and the Metropole Hotel. London contractors Messrs Jennings & Co built the Metropole Hotel in 1896-7 on what was the Polo Field, and the whole undertaking took about 20 months. The Metropole Hotel Company, which was originally set-up to build the hotel, sold out to Gordon Hotels just before completion, the hotel opened on 1 July 1897.

West Leas and the Metropole Hotel in October 2001. On 16 October 1959 Mrs Watkins purchased from Gordon Hotels the lease of the Metropole for £51,000. Her plan was to convert the hotel into 39 flats. The new owners were the Glanmoor Management Company Ltd. By mid 1962 all the flats were let and the building was known as the New Metropole. In the present day the Metropole Galleries and a health and leisure club occupy the ground-floor public rooms.

An aerial view of the centre of Folkestone in 1956, showing the large hotels in the foreground, and the famous Leas Cliff Hall (concert hall, ballroom, restaurant) on the edge of the cliff overlooking the sea. The building behind the Leas Cliff Hall with the curved roof is the Pleasure Gardens Theatre, and the tall chimney behind the Pleasure Gardens belongs to the Electricity Company's generating station at Morehall.

Lower Sandgate Road and Sea Front

THE area known as The Under Cliff (Lower Sandgate Road) was formed in 1784 by a major landslip, which ran the length of the coast from the Harbour towards Sandgate. This created an undulating ribbon of land a few metres wide that could no longer be used for arable farming. Subsequently the land has remained in this form to the present day with only minor changes made due to coastal defence work. After the development of the harbour, Lord Radnor developed a toll road between the harbour and Sandgate, on top of the landslip known as the Lower Sandgate Road. By 1820 the road had a small wooden tollhouse with a tall brick chimney. In 1847 the present-day building of Kentish rag stone and brick replaced the original wooden tollhouse.

A series of paths were constructed by 1877. The 2nd Edition Ordnance Survey Map of 1898 shows numerous paths descending from the Leas Shelter and also meandering the Toll Road from the Toll House, eastwards towards Marine Terrace.

Moving further east, the development of a gas works was completed on the beach in 1842. The building of Marine Terrace commenced in 1860. The gas works was moved to Foord road in 1866 and the site was used to build Marine Crescent. The Bathing Establishment (Marina) opened in 1869. The Victoria Pier and Switchback Railway opened in 1888. The Folkestone Rowing Club was formed 1874 and their club house on the Lower Sandgate Road was completed in 1884. In 1893 the Marine Gardens Bandstand was erected and the Lower Sandgate Road gardens were laid out. The Folkestone lifeboat station was established in 1893 with a boathouse next to the rowing club. The first part of Marine Promenade was built in 1910. During World War One the Marine Parade and gardens were used to build rest camps.

In 1935-6 Lord Radnor decided to clean up the beach, so he built a horseshoe of huts for the boatmen which was followed by the building of an open-air swimming pool, the Rotunda Amusement Park, and boating pool, followed in the 1950s by an open-air skating rink.

From 1913 to 1973 the Radnor Estate leased the Lower Leas Park to the Council, retaining the tolls gathered from the road. Due to falling revenue the Estate sold the area to the Council in 1973 and ceased to collect the tolls. The toll road then became a no-through road and footpath, and the Lower Leas finally became a proper park, closed to traffic. The Toll House was left vacant until 1980 when it was sold into private ownership.

Apart from the Rotunda the other amenities were swept away in the 1980s to erect fair ground rides and another amusement arcade. The open-air swimming pool closed in 1981 and was filled in, to accommodate an outdoor Sunday market and car park, which opened in 1982.

On 27 May 2000 a new Coastal Leisure Park costing £1 million was opened along the Lower Sandgate Road between the Zig-Zag Path and the Tollgate. It consists of a children's fun zone with extensive play equipment and a 150-seat amphitheatre.

The Tollgate looking west: after the development of the harbour, Lord Radnor developed a toll road between the harbour and Sandgate known as the Lower Sandgate Road. By 1820 the road had a small wooden tollhouse with a tall brick chimney. In 1847 the wooden tollhouse was replace by this building of Kentish rag stone and brick.

The present-day tollhouse is in private ownership, but from 1913 to 1973 the Radnor Estate leased the Lower Leas Park to the Council, retaining the tolls gathered from the road. Due to falling revenue the Estate sold the area to the Council in 1973 and ceased to collect the tolls. The toll road then became a no-through road and it closed to traffic.

The Lower Sandgate Road and tollhouse looking east: it is interesting to note the tollgate is open allowing a horse-drawn carriage to pass though. The last tolls before they ceased being collected in 1973 were: Motor Car 10p, Motor Cycle with Sidecar 2p, Motor Cycle 2p, and Bicycle, Horse or Handcart p.

The Lower Sandgate Road looking east: the western end of the new Coastal Park can just be seen through the tollgates. The new leisure park with its fun zone for children and amphitheatre was opened on Saturday 27 May 2000 by celebrity weatherman Ian Macaskill. The tollgate cottage (to the right of picture) was sold during the middle of 2001. It was on the market for £265,000.

LOWER SANDGATE ROAD AND SEA FRONT

The Lower Sandgate Road looking west in Edwardian times: this area known as the Under Cliff, was formed in 1784 by a major landslip. This created an undulating ribbon of land a few metres wide that could no longer be used for arable farming. Subsequently the land has remained in this form to the present day with only minor changes due to coastal defence work.

The eastern end of the new Coastal Park, Lower Sandgate Road, seen here just over a year after it was opened. Part of the children's fun zone with its extensive play equipment can be seen at the end of the road. The 150-seat grass amphitheatre is to the east of this photograph at the bottom of the Zig-Zag path.

Marine Walk, Victoria Pier and Switchback Railway in about 1910: the foundation stone for the Victoria Pier was laid on Saturday 7 May 1887 by Viscountess Folkestone. She also opened the pier on 21 July 1888. Thompson's Gravity Switchback Co Ltd patented the Switchback Railway; it was constructed in 1888 and commenced operating on Friday 17 August the same year. The Marine walk opened in 1906.

Marine Walk in October 2001: the Switchback Railway was constantly being damaged by storms and after its closure during World War One, the damage was so extensive that it was demolished and the timber was sold to an Ashford timber merchants. The Victoria Pier Pavilion was burnt out on Whit Monday 1945. The pier was demolished in 1952-3 after standing derelict for five years.

The Leas Lift was designed and built in 1885 by R.G. Waygood at a cost of about £3,000, and was officially opened on 21 September 1885. It became so popular that five years later in 1890 a second lift was installed. The second lift, removed in 1985, ran on the adjacent track and its cars were of a most unusual design, having stepped seats one above the other, as can be seen in the photograph.

The Leas Lift today operates from Easter to October, 9am to 6pm daily; and from October onwards, Sundays only (weather permitting). My photograph shows two sets of tracks; the left one (1885) is the only track in use now. The Leas Lift is the only one driven by water balance that still survives on the south coast. The television series *The Darling Buds of May*, whilst filming in Folkestone, used the lift in one of their episodes. Filmed by the Yorkshire Television crew on 1 June 1991. The stars David Jason, Philip Franks, Pam Ferris, Anna Massey, Moray Watson and Catherine Zeta-Jones were all present.

The seafront in the early 1890s. On the extreme left, the building with the rustic fence is the Folkestone Rowing Club headquarters, built in 1884 at a cost of £300; next to it is a camera obscurer. Bathing machines can be seen further along the beach just above the high water mark, they include Fagg's Patent Bathing Machine, at this time it was an offence to undress on the beach. The building at the end of Marine Terrace with the clock tower is the Harbour Company's office; it was built in 1843 and demolished in 1899.

The seafront has seen many changes down the years, the lifeboat station closed in 1930 and the boathouse was demolished in 1935. The rowing club moved their headquarters to Sandgate in 1946. In 1981 the open-air swimming pool closed and was filled in to provide space for a Sunday market and car park. After the acquisition by Jimmy Godden of 19 acres of seafront (including the Rotunda amusement park), in 1983, the boating pool was filled in, and the skating rink and fishermen's huts were dispensed with, to provide space for more fair ground rides. A second domed arcade similar to the Rotunda was added in 1984. The Marine Gardens Shelter, which opened on 2 June 1906 was converted in 1984 and demolished in 1987.

The Lower Sandgate Road and Marine Parade before World War One. The building of Marine Terrace commenced in 1860 (the buildings with the sign on the gable), the Marine Gardens (centre of picture) were laid out in 1892, and the Marine Gardens Bandstand (the building with the pointed roof) was erected in 1893 and demolished in 1927. After the disposal of bathing machines bathing cabins were built on the beach for the use of bathers. These bathing cabins can be seen on the right of the picture.

The Hotel Burstin dominates this modern picture of the Lower Sandgate Road and Marine Parade. A seafront facelift in 1992 included the planting of 64 palm trees and thousands of sub-tropical plants, some of which can be seen on the left. On the right can be seen some of the rides in the amusement park, and the fishing boat *Accord* which was added to the attractions in February 1998. Most of the buildings in Marine Crescent (left foreground) are not occupied, the windows are boarded-up and they are waiting to be converted into luxury flats.

The Lower Sandgate Road and seafront in 1889. Both the Victoria Pier and Switchback Railway, which opened in 1888, are very evident in this picture. The photograph was taken just four years before the Marine Gardens were laid out, making the beach look very wide. The official high water mark was on the landside of Marine Parade, I was told by an old boatman 'Jacko' Fagg, that in bad weather he had seen seawater reach the bottom of the Road of Remembrance. The first stage of the pier development built in 1861 can be seen in the distance, with either the paddle steamer *Duchess of York* or *Princess of Wales* approaching. It is interesting to note the vegetable patch in the right-hand corner of the picture.

Today's picture tells quite a different story. The gardens in the Lower Sandgate Road as seen here, were laid out in 1893, and the Marine Gardens were laid in 1892. But the Marine Gardens have not survived in their original form; they are now covered with fairground rides, a crazy golf course, and ice-cream kiosks. It is interesting to note that the amusement park has spread onto the beach, the plans were passed in 1986 and in 1992 a new promenade was built on the sea side of the fairground rides.

In this 1930s postcard, all the amenities built on the beach after Lord Radnor's 'great clean-up' are in place. The open-air seawater bathing pool was opened on 11 July 1936, while the boating pool, its restaurant and Rotunda opened in 1937. Between the boating pool and bathing pool there is a horseshoe of huts built by Lord Radnor for the fishermen. In the right foreground can be seen the rowing club headquarters.

This present-day photograph is dominated by two large open spaces, which were formally the sites of the bathing pool, skating rink and horseshoe of huts. The space in the foreground is a car park; the second space is used for the Sunday market. The building between them has survived as a café from the bathing pool days. The building with the domed roof was built in 1984 as an amusement arcade.

The Harbour

A REFERENCE from Hasted's *History of Kent* (1790) states: "There are now eight or ten lugger-boats and cutters, employed chiefly in the herring and mackerel fisheries, besides about 30 small-boats employed in the same, and in the catching of plaice, sole, whiting, skate, and such kind of fish, in their proper seasons which altogether employ between 200 and 300 men and boys. The fish are conveyed to the London markets, either by boats, or by land carriage."

There was a time when Folkestone's Stade had no sea defences and boats were pulled up on to the open beach. The area was periodically hit by severe storms with loss of life, beach, boats and damage to fishermen's houses.

In 1804 Lord Radnor petitioned Parliament for the construction of a stone harbour. The new harbour, built of local sand stone, was completed in 1810 and reached its final form in 1905 following development by the South-Eastern and Chatham Railway.

In 1843 trains were delivering passengers to the new Folkestone-Boulogne ferry service.

In 1849 some 49,000 passengers had used Folkestone harbour, and by 1903, 208,000 passengers and 70,000 tons of cargo were dealt with at the port.

The Stade (landing place) has been used by fishermen for over 1,300 years, but it was not until 1860 that the quay was built and a new fish market was opened on 2 August 1862. The South-Eastern Railway Company had their marine workshops and jetty at the eastern end of the outer harbour, it closed and moved to Dover in 1922.

By the mid-18th century Folkestone harbour had a flourishing cargo trade importing coal, timber, and ice and exporting chalk (for lime burning). These cargoes were usually unloaded at the inner harbour. Many of the sailing ships, brigs, brigantines or spritsail barges were registered at Folkestone and were owned by local business people. By the 1920s most of the cargo trade had transferred to steam ships, which mainly used the outer harbour, the inner harbour was then used for private vessels.

During World War One (1914-18) the harbour was the main embarkation point for British troops bound for the Western front, some 10,463,834 military mailbags were handled. In addition to the troops 120,000 refugees passed through the port.

During the World War Two the port was closed to civilian traffic. After the Dunkirk evacuation (26 May-4 June) 44,000 personnel came through the port, they were sent inland on 80 trains.

In 1945 cargo services to Calais resumed and on 1 October to Belgium. On 1 August 1946 the SS *Auto Carrier* commenced a service to Boulogne for cars.

1 July 1947 saw the restoration of the Folkestone-Boulogne service, 67,287 passengers had used the route by 4 October when the service was suspended for the winter.

In 1960 the Boulogne, Calais and Ostend routes carried: 839,392 passengers, 438 cars and 276 commercial vehicles. In 1971-2, work commenced on the erection of new buildings and a car ramp to handle Ro-Ro (Roll on Roll off) traffic. Two new ships the *Hengist* and *Horsa* were built for the service.

In 1972 the Boulogne, Calais and Ostend services carried: 1,266,783 passengers, 913,160 cars, 5,633 commercial vehicles and 31,594 freight vehicles. In 1985 Sealink, a subsidiary of British Rail, was privatised from which time there have been various ferry operators, including a Seacat, until the middle of the year 2001, when commercial links with the continent were severed.

The fishing industry has been declining for many years, partly due to the lack of fish and EU regulations. At present there are just 10 fishing boats and 30 men employed in the industry.

The harbour from the Bayle: showing the inner harbour thronged with sailing ships unloading their cargoes of timber or coal. Those that are moored stern to the quay have a plank of wood, from the ship to the shore, used to walk on while carrying cargo ashore by hand. The clock tower on the right of the picture belongs to the Pavilion Hotel.

I was in a very precarious position taking this photograph, as I could not get near the edge of the cliff. I climbed the cliff from the Bayle steps, taking this photograph through the trees. In the earlier picture the branch line to the Harbour is a timber structure including the swing bridge, while in the modern picture it is built of brick, and the swing bridge (installed in 1930) is steel. The swing bridge has only been opened a few times since World War Two and it is now fixed.

The inner harbour looking towards Harbour Street in about 1912. In those days the inner basin was very commercialised as seen in the picture. Many of these sailing ships, brigs and brigantines, were registered at Folkestone, owned by local traders and manned by local seamen. On the left of the picture can be seen the Pavilion Hotel followed by the County Skating Rink and the London and Paris Hotel.

Private vessels have used the inner harbour since the 1920s when the cargo trade for the sailing vessels started to be taken over by steam ships. The site of the County Skating Rink is now a car park and the London and Paris Hotel has been, renamed Gillespie's.

The harbour and pier just after World War One. The pier as we see it here was built between 1897 and 1905, the inner end of the pier (out to the knuckle) was built behind the old wooden pier built in 1861. The large two-storey building on the South Quay is the Custom House, which was built in 1854, and the building to its left is a freight shed. It is interesting to note that there are two passenger ferries and one cargo ship on the east side of the pier and one passenger ferry on the west side.

The present-day scene at the harbour is rather sad and somewhat different to the previous one. The cranes have been removed, a car ferry ramp has been built along with a customs clearing shed for cars and one for foot passengers, but alas there are no ferries to be seen. The last ship to run from Folkestone was a freight ship, which ceased running in the middle of 2001 when commercial links with the continent were severed.

A 1930s view of the inner harbour: the two boats in front of the slipway, formerly lifeboats, are the *Ocean King* and the *Viking*, they were both used as pleasure boats taking visitors for trips round the bay. Most of the buildings in Beach Street and Harbour Street seen in the picture were ether demolished or badly damaged in World War Two by a parachute mine on 18 November 1940.

The number of pleasure boats seen here in the inner harbour, illustrates the sign of the times, the affluent public have more disposable money to spend on their leisure. It is interesting to note that most of the buildings seen in the previous picture have gone, and that modern blocks of flats dominate the skyline.

THE HARBOUR

The outer harbour from the South Quay looking towards the Stade in about 1902. In the foreground is the *Robbie Burns* brigantine built in Canada in 1868. The vessel was sold to the French in 1905. Behind her is another sailing ship, followed by the cargo steamer *Canterbury*. The paddle steamer with the two bell funnels is either the *Princess of Wales* or the *Duchess of York*.

The outer harbour in October 2001: rather a different story to the congested scene in the last picture. The buildings along the Stade were built in 1935-6 and replaced the earlier ones. Fish shed number one, is now occupied by Folkestone Trawlers Fish Shop to the right of which can be seen the Oddfellows Arms (1843) whose successor has just been refurbished and reopened as the Front.

An aerial view of the harbour and town c.1950; the turbine steamship at the pier, in number one berth, is either the *Canterbury* or *Isle of Thanet*, and in number two berth is one of the Southern Railway Company's cargo ships. On the left of the picture can be seen the burnt-out remains of the Victoria Pier, the open air bathing pool, the boating lake and Rotunda amusement arcade. The 19-arch railway viaduct built in 1843 to span the Foord Valley is very prominent in the right of the picture.

The outer harbour and fishing fleet in the mid-1930s, all these fishing smacks were originally sailing luggers they started to have engines fitted after World War One. When a fisherman has nothing to do, he invariably looks out-to-sea as these two seen here leaning on the lamp-post, the one on the left is Albert 'Nobby' Taylor.

The present-day fishing fleet in the Outer Harbour: these boats are mostly built of fibreglass or steel, whereas the old luggers were all timber. The methods of fishing have also changed, today they mostly fish with trawl or gill nets, crab pots and whelk nets, where as the luggers mostly went long-lining and drift-net fishing.

The fish market and Stade in the 1890s: when there were 50 large boats and many small ones constantly engaged in the fisheries. It is interesting to note the absence of railings along the quayside. There are three fish sheds along the Stade and the railway lines leading to the South-Eastern Railway Company's Marine Workshops. The two buildings, with the pointed gable ends are the Jubilee Inn and Odd Fellows Arms and the large weather-boarded building is Mr T.H. Franks, sail-making workshop.

The transformation of the Stade took place in 1935-6, when the old fishermen's houses and pubs were demolished and replaced with the ones seen here. Numbers two and three fish sheds have also been demolished. The remaining fish shed was converted into a fish shop opening on 11 December 1985 by Folkestone Trawlers Ltd. The net pots seen here on the slipway are for catching crabs and lobsters.

These weather-boarded buildings were originally built for storing drift nets, but at the time this photograph was taken they were being used as general stores and fish wholesaler's offices. All these buildings survived the general clearance scheme of 1935-6, except for the old tanlade on the right hand side of the picture, which was demolished to extend the fish store of Arthur Goddard, fish wholesaler, and a new tanlade was built in East Street.

The modern picture, taken in October 2001, of the buildings at the Stade, is not so impressive as the one of days gone by. The business of A. Goddard & Son, fish wholesalers, was established in 1899, it closed on 21 December 1991 after which the building fell into disrepair before being refurbished in 2000 and opening as The Stade Fish Bar. The next building, with the hung tiles, is the fish store and offices of Folkestone Trawlers Ltd.

THE HARBOUR

The fishing lugger *FE243* is seen here entering the outer harbour in the 1890s after a tides fishing. As the vessel was moving fast enough with the wind behind her, the crew are dropping the sails while entering the harbour. The left hand vessel of the two with funnels is the *Jubilee Life Saving Ship number one*. She was designed for saving life at sea, but she was also used for the transportation of perishable goods to and from Boulogne.

The outer harbour seen here from the South Quay in October 2001. There are now only 10 commercial fishing boats fishing out of Folkestone, employing about 30 men in the industry. The houses on the Stade, built in 1935-6 consist of two uniform terraces, unlike the fishermen's houses in the earlier photograph.

The outer harbour seen here from the East Cliff in about 1880. In the foreground can be seen the South-Eastern Railway Company's Marine Workshops and repair jetty. It is interesting to note the paddle steamer out of the water, she is one of the earlier type built of timber with a clipper bow; she is seen here on the gridiron undergoing repairs. The South-Eastern and Chatham Railway Company closed these workshops in 1922 consolidating their ship repair work at Dover.

The outer harbour, seen here from the East Cliff, is mainly used by fishing boats and a few yachts that appear in the summertime. The large white building, dominating the skyline on the right of the picture, is the Burstin Hotel, formerly the site of the Pavilion Hotel. The building in the foreground with the white gable is Sea Point, a complex of 18 flats and maisonettes, which replaced the Sunny Sands Restaurant.

East Cliff and Warren

IN 1924 Lord Radnor gave for the enjoyment of the town the East Cliff area. This extended the amenities of the resort considerably, and the East Cliff, which had previously been arable farming land, began to develop. The East Cliff Pavilion was built and new lawns were laid out. The East Cliff sands were improved by the removal of rocks, and the cliff was landscaped with terraced walks and flower beds. In 1935 a new promenade was constructed and called Coronation Parade. A remarkable attraction was revealed in 1924 when a portion of the cliffs at East Wear Bay collapsed, it revealed the site of a Roman Villa. Roman remains were discovered on East Cliff, and they proved to be a major attraction, hundreds of visitors wandered round the foundations. The site stimulated a keen interest in local history, and but for the coming of World War Two, would have been a permanent asset to the town. But the site received considerable damage during the war, which prompted the council to have the site filled in; and much of it still remains under the turf beside the Wear Bay Road.

Just east of Folkestone there lays an area of under cliff landscape known as the Warren. It is renowned for its spectacular scenery, wild life, and variety of flora and fauna.

The main railway from Folkestone to Dover runs through the Warren, the South-Eastern Railway opened it in 1844. In 1884 the SER decided to open a small station in the heart of the Warren, for they were well aware of the appeal of the area to ramblers. The line has been plagued with landslips ever since it was opened. In 1920 the Warren was taken over by the Folkestone Corporation from its owner Lord Radnor. Subsequently the Corporation undertook the construction of broad footpaths giving easy access into the region, facilities for camping, and a bathing station were built, while at the same time new sea defence work, was carried out by the railway company. In 1948 due to the forward movement of the sea wall at the Warren Halt area, stabilisation work by way of two large aprons were built and this type of construction work has continued eastwards over the years.

The development of Wear Bay Road from Dover Road continued after World War Two, into the 1950s and 1960s. In 1961 the railway line between Folkestone and Dover was electrified and the Warren Halt was reserved solely for engineers.

The Warren remains comparatively unspoilt and is now protected and managed as a nature reserve attracting ramblers and naturalists as well as campers and day-trippers.

The East Cliff Sands the harbour, seafront and town, looking west in c.1948. On the extreme left of the picture, a pre-cast concrete wall is being built and behind it the ground is being levelled off. During World War Two there was a slipway built there for the use of amphibious ducks. Note the railway sidings on the west side of the Harbour, the seafront as built in the mid-1930s, and the burnt-out Victoria Pier. Note the Harbour Street and the Beach Street areas, flattened by a parachute mine during Word War Two. The buildings with the arches at the bottom of the Old High Street are on the west side of Harbour Street backing onto South Street, and they were demolished c.1950. The path running along the top of East Cliff has now disappeared down the cliff; these cliffs are prone to slipping during wet weather due to a clay belt, which runs through the East Cliff.

The Bathing Beach at the East Cliff looking east in the 1920s. In 1924 Lord Radnor gave the East Cliff area to the town to extend the amenities. At the time this picture was taken some of the rocks had been clear away to make a sandy beach and the corporation had installed a boatman to watch over the bathers (seen here in the rowing boat).

The East Cliff Sands in October 2001, a rather deserted scene compared to the earlier one. In the mid-1920s a promenade stretching halfway along the beach was erected, it was succeeded in 1935 by the Coronation Parade and still exists today. The unusually-shaped building at the foot of the cliffs is one of Southern Water's pumping stations, completed in 2000.

The East Cliff Sands and Sunny Sands Restaurant: in about 1965. The sandy beach is a playground for holidaymakers and locals alike, where families enjoy swimming or just lazing in the sun. The Sunny Sands Restaurant was built in 1960, on the site of the former South-Eastern Railway Company's Marine Workshops, which closed in 1922 and were purchased by the Council from the Southern Railway in 1927 for £3,200. The council used the workshops for bathing cabins etc.

The present-day: East Cliff Sands and East Cliff, looking east. Due to the lack of demand and shorter holiday seasons the Sunny Sands Restaurant was demolished to make way for this complex of flats and maisonettes called Harbour Point.

The East Cliff Sands looking west in 1927. Many of the rocks have been cleared away from the beach and a promenade has been built to create a pleasure beach. In 1935 the promenade was replaced with the Coronation Parade as seen today. At the end of the Stade can be seen the bathing cabins, formerly the South-Eastern Railway Company's Marine Workshops.

The present-day view, of the East Cliff Sands looking west. There are six major changes that have taken place since the earlier photograph was taken, they are: the building of; Coronation Parade, the Pumping Station, Harbour Point flats, the Burstin Hotel, number one The Leas (flats) and Boots the Chemists.

The East Cliff in the early 1920s, when most of the area was still arable farming land. In 1924 Lord Radnor gave this area for the enjoyment of the town, this extended the amenities of the resort considerably, and the East Cliff, began to develop. The building with the pointed roof to the left of the lamp-post is where the East Cliff Pavilion was built.

The East Cliff has been transformed almost beyond recognition since the 1920s. Most of the houses were built in the 1930s. The Council built the East Cliff Pavilion in 1934 to expand the facilities for entertainment in the town. It is now privately owned and is called the Pavilion. Many paths and lawns have been laid out and the grassed area by Martello Tower number three is a pitch-and-putt golf course.

Martello Tower number one, path to the Valiant Sailor public house, and entrance to the Warren c.1914. Due to the threat of an invasion early in the 19th century by Napoleon, 74 Martello Towers, such as these, were built between 1805 and 1808 stretching from Folkestone to Seaford, the one in the picture being the first.

The present-day picture of the path to the Valiant Sailor and entrance to the Warren is not so rugged as the early one. The road illustrated here was built c.1947 to give access to the Warren foreshore for the contractors working on the sea defences. On the left can be seen a house which is on the post-war Hollands Avenue Estate.

The East Cliff in the 1920s, taken from the access to the Warren, looking southwest. In the foreground is Martello Tower number-one, on the right of which can be seen the Warren Farm, run by Edwin Burbidge, a dairyman who also had a shop at 10 Beach Street.

Today Martello Tower number-one is occupied; it has been completely restored and converted into a house. The walls facing the sea are 13ft thick while the landward side are 6ft; the whole of the outside skin of brickwork has been rebuilt. The two houses seen in the middle distance are in Wear Bay Road and were built in 1957.

This aerial view, taken in 1950 looking north-east, is of the Wear Bay Road area and the Warren. It is interesting to note that much of Foreland Avenue and Warren Way have not been developed, White Cliff Way has not been built and that there are no houses in Wear Bay Road from Foreland Avenue heading north. The large concrete apron seen on the Warren foreshore was built in 1948 to stop the forward movement of the sea wall, which had moved seaward one metre since being built in the 1920s.

The Folkestone Warren from East Wear Bay looking towards Dover. The photograph was taken before 1920 when the Folkestone Corporation took over control of the Warren from its owner Lord Radnor. When the tide is out, as illustrated here, one can glean fossils from the foreshore. The outcrop just west of East Wear Bay was the site of a major industry in pre-Roman times, the rocks were fashioned into milling stones called querns, the remains of which can to this day still sometimes be found.

The Warren today has a caravan park and a campsite, and is protected and managed as a nature reserve attracting ramblers and naturalists as well as campers and day-trippers. There is a continuous sea wall from East Wear Bay to Abbots Cliff to stop the erosion by the sea in order to protect the main railway line from Folkestone to Dover.

East Wear Bay in about 1925: just after the Council had taken possession of the Warren, whence they undertook the construction of broad footpaths giving easy access into the region. The bathing cabins seen here were built c.1922 but they only survived a few years before being destroyed by storms.

East Wear Bay and the Warren as can be seen today. The sea wall was built in about 1926 to stop cliff erosion by the sea. The buttresses seen here were built about ten years later to stop the sea wall moving seawards. It is interesting to note that there is a lot more tree-cover now than in the earlier picture.

Places of Entertainment

PLACES of entertainment in Folkestone from the Victorian era included the Town Hall; and for its first opening in 1861 the main hall was booked for Choral Society concerts, penny readings, Christy's Minstrels, amateur theatricals and balls, all of which were frequently repeated. The Pleasure Gardens Theatre opened in 1888 as the Exhibition Palace Theatre; the building was originally built for the Arts Treasures Exhibition of 1886. The Bathing Establishment opened in 1869 was later renamed the Marina. The Leas Shelter opened in 1894 as a concert hall. The Victoria Pier Pavilion opened in 1888. The Leas Pavilion was opened as a superior tearoom on 1 July 1902. The Electric Theatre opened in 1910 was later to be called the Savoy. The Playhouse, Central and Queen's cinemas all opened in 1912 respectively.

World War One had devastating effects on the more exclusive end of the holiday market, the upper class didn't return in their pre-war numbers, so the town broadened its appeal and tried to make itself more inviting to attract the middle class. In 1925 work commenced on the refurbishment and extension of the Leas Shelter to become the present-day Leas Cliff Hall, which was opened by Prince Henry of Tech on 13 July 1927. In 1928 Jimmy Grant Anderson built a stage at the Leas Pavilion and introduced plays and tea matinees and in 1929 the Arthur Brough Players moved in.

Two more concert halls and one cinema were also built. The Marine Gardens Pavilion (1926) the East Cliff Pavilion (1934), and the Astoria cinema (1935).

The slogan 'Floral Folkestone' was also introduced with the opening of Kingsnorth Gardens and by laying out attractive flowerbeds in Sandgate Road, the Leas, Radnor Park and elsewhere around the town. Folkestone once again became a popular holiday destination.

But the town suffered heavy damage from shelling and bombing in World War Two. The Victoria Pier Pavilion was badly damaged by fire on Whit Monday in 1945; it never re-opened and was subsequently demolished in 1952-3.

Once again (as was the case after World War One) following the cessation of hostilities in 1945 holidaymakers did not return in great numbers and subsequently the town went into a downward spiral. In 1961 the Savoy cinema introduced Bingo sessions and it became the Star Social Club, this was due to the decline in patrons accelerated by television. In September 1990 the building opened as the Metronome concert hall, but closed just four months later. The building still remains empty to this day. The Playhouse cinema closed in 1962 and the Pleasure Gardens Theatre ceased having live entertainment in 1956 and became a full time cinema. This was not a success and the building closed in May 1964 and demolition followed the same year. The end for the Odeon cinema came on 26 January 1974 with a double James Bond presentation. The building was subsequently demolished. In September 1985 the Leas Pavilion closed and re-opened in March 1986 as the Leas Club, by its present owners the Warburton family. The Cannon cinema formally the Central closed in 1988 leaving the town at that time without a cinema. The Marine Gardens Pavilion became privately owned and opened as the La Parisienne nightclub in 1988, currently The Beach and Indigo nightclubs.

The Silver Screen Cinema Company opened a multi-screen cinema in the former Council Chamber of the Old Town Hall on 20 April 1990, with the films *Hunt for Red October* – starring Sean Connery – and the Oscar-winning *Driving Miss Daisy*.

PLACES OF ENTERTAINMENT

The Bathing Establishment, Lower Sandgate Road was opened July 1869. The building was designed by Joseph Gardner and was commenced in 1867. It was one of the earliest seaside attractions in Folkestone and soon became popular with the increasing numbers of visitors to the town. Its facilities included hot and cold baths, medicated baths, vapour baths, a swimming pool, reception and refreshment rooms, billiard room, reading room and a large saloon with balcony. An extension was added to the front, as can be seen here, to accommodate a larger swimming pool, it was later covered over and used as a dance floor.

After World War Two the Marina gradually went into decline, it closed in 1958, except for the swimming pool, which was sublet to Folkestone Corporation and run by Sam Rocket, a former cross-Channel swimmer. In 1965 following considerable damage by vandals the pool closed. The Council considered various proposals for the Marina but lacking the finance to purchase, the building was demolished in 1966 and the site has been used as a temporary car park ever since.

This building built by the Folkestone Art Treasures Exhibition Company in Bouverie Road West, was opened on 15 May 1886, the project did not obtain the expected support, and closed after five months. Two years later (1888) it changed hands and became the property of the Folkestone Exhibition Palace Company. Soon after the name was changed to the Pleasure Gardens Theatre, and the 16 acres of ground were laid out for tennis, hockey, croquet and skating, and there was a rustic bandstand. A weekly programme of plays, operas, Shakespearean productions, romantic comedies, revues and musical shows were presented all the year round.

The Pleasure Gardens Theatre ceased having live entertainment in 1956 and became a full time cinema, this was not a success and the building closed in May 1964, and it was demolished the same year. This complex of offices were built on the site and were occupied by the Orion Insurance Company in September 1968, they were taken over by Guardian Health who moved out in 1999. The building is now Folkestone's police station; the force moved in on Tuesday 23 October 2000.

PLACES OF ENTERTAINMENT

The Leas Shelter was erected by the Earl of Radnor and leased to the Corporation for 21 years from 25 March 1894, at a rent of £85 10s per annum. The Folkestone Amusements Association ran the building. It contained a 62ft by 31ft central hall where an orchestra played daily. The building had a spacious balcony where visitors could read their papers or enjoy the superb sea views under the glass canopy and listen to the light music of the band.

In 1924 it was decided that a larger and more majestic hall was required, work began on a new building in 1925. The Leas Cliff Hall was designed by Mr J.S. Dahi; the main contractor was J. Godden and Son builders, from Ham Street. The building cost £80,000 to build. Prince Henry of Tech opened it on 13 July 1927.

The Electric Theatre opened in Grace Hill on Tuesday 3 May 1910, it was renamed the Savoy in 1928 when talking films were installed. The ornamental glass canopy was a feature particularly favoured by the architect A.R. Bowles and it appeared in other halls of the period.

In October 1961 the Savoy cinema introduced bingo sessions and it became the Star Social Club, which closed in 1963. The building remained unoccupied until September 1990 when it opened as the Metronome concert hall. This venture was not successful and the hall closed just four months later and remains empty to this day.

The Central Picture Theatre in George Lane was built in 1912; it was designed by the architect H. Vivian. The Central had a canopied entrance under which was a centrally sited exterior pay box, patrons having bought their ticket could proceed to a tea and refreshment bar. The 85ft auditorium seated 750 people. The opening attraction for the week commencing 23 September 1912 was a 'colossal cine drama' entitled *The Mysteries of Paris*, live music being presented by the resident Arcadians Orchestra.

The Cannon Cinema, formally the Central, closed in 1988 leaving the town without a cinema. The building was demolished in December 1988 and January 1989 the site is now occupied by a complex of small shop units with flats over. Today the Bayle Community Centre occupies part of the cinema site.

The Playhouse Cinema, Guildhall Street, was designed by A.R. Bowles, the building was faced with Bath stone, it had a glass canopy under which was a marble floor. The cinema seated 732 people. The architect originally envisaged permission for a 1,000-seat theatre, but the Town Council vetoed this. The Playhouse opened on Wednesday 14 August 1912. The programme of silent pictures included an early version of *Treasure Island*. Talking pictures were not featured regularly until December 1929.

The Playhouse closed in 1962 and the building was demolished the following year. Today Peacocks clothing store, formerly Tesco Stores Ltd, now occupies the site.

The Astoria Cinema was designed by the architect E.A. Stone the main contractor was the local builder O. Marx. The cost of the building was £55,000 exclusive of the site. The Astoria opened on Saturday 20 April 1935. The opening film was *The Gay Divorce*, staring Fred Astaire and Ginger Rogers, which ran for eight days. After a company merger the Odeon sign replaced the Astoria in 1940. This photograph was taken in 1937 for Folkestone's Floral Festival.

The end of the Odeon Cinema came on 26 January 1974 with a double James Bond bill. The Odeon was demolished in November and December of that year. Today the site is occupied by Boots the Chemist. It is interesting to note that while the builders were digging out the footings for Boots, formerly the site of Carlo Mastrani's restaurant (before the Astoria), they came across Carlo Mastrani's nougat-making machine, apparently he was noted for his nougat.

Churches and Chapels

THE Parish Church of SS Mary and Eanswythe was founded in 1137 by Nigel de Muneville and is a cruciform building of Kentish ragstone, chiefly in the Early English style with later insertions, and has a central tower of perpendicular date containing a clock and eight bells: there is a fine altar-tomb, with an effigy. As Folkestone began to expand so too was there a need for more places to worship, by the year 1900 the following churches for all denominations had been built.

Christ Church in Sandgate Road was an ecclesiastical parish, formed in 1851: the church, consecrated on 27 July 1850, was built of Kentish rag with Bath stone dressings in a plain Gothic style, and has a tower containing one bell.

The Congregational Church, Tontine Street opened on 18 August 1857.

The Wesleyan Methodists Church was built on Grace Hill in 1864. It was built of stone in Early English style, the tower being surmounted by a graceful spire. The church opened on 31 March 1866.

Holy Trinity is an ecclesiastical parish formed in 1868: the church, partially erected in 1868, and completed in 1889, is a cruciform edifice of rag stone with Bath stone, built in Early English style, and has a central octagonal tower with spire containing one bell.

The Baptist Church at Rendezvous Street was built in the Italian style, but the ornamentation of the façade is Corinthian, it opened on 4 August 1874.

St John the Baptist's Church, St John's Church Road, was built in Early English style and opened in 1879.

St Michael and All Angels was built in 1873 it was of red brick, in the Flamboyant style, and had a tower with spire, containing eight tubular bells.

St Peter's, East Cliff, is an ecclesiastical parish formed 13 November 1868: the church, erected in 1855 is of Kentish rag stone in the Early English style, and has a turret containing one bell.

The Emmanuel Proprietary Church in Cheriton Road was built in 1882; it is a plain brick building and was erected under a trust deed, which, during the lease, provided services of strictly Evangelical character.

St Saviour's Church is an ecclesiastical parish formed 21 August 1885, from the parishes of St Mary and St Michael and All Angels: the church in Canterbury Road was opened in June 1892. A tower was never built because the vicar regarded it as a useless expense. Instead, a bell-turret housing three bells was built on the gabled west end in 1899.

The Roman Catholic Church in Guildhall Street, dedicated to Our Lady Help of Christians and St Aloysius, was erected in 1889 and is of local brick with Bath stone dressings, in the Early Gothic style.

The Congregational Mission Hall & School of Canterbury Road was built in red brick with Bath stone dressings and opened on 12 July 1893.

The Congregational Church, Radnor Park (United Reform), was built in 1896 in the Gothic style of the Early Decorated period.

There was also a number of smaller places of worship including; the Primitive Methodist Church in Dover Street, the Friends' Meeting House also in Dover Street, the Ebenezer Mission Room in Rossendale Road, the Zion (Strict Baptist) Chapel at St Michael's Street, a Mission Hall and School in North Street, the Church of the Good Shepherd in Victoria Grove, St Augustine's Mission Church in Mill Bay, The Victoria Hall Cheriton Road, the Fishermen's Bethel in The Stade, the Tabernacle, Harvey Street, The Christian Science Reading Room in Christ Church Road and the Railway Mission Hall, St John's Street.

Due to the decline in people attending church, and also the spiralling cost of maintaining Victorian churches, a number have been demolished or put to other uses and in some instances new modern churches have been built.

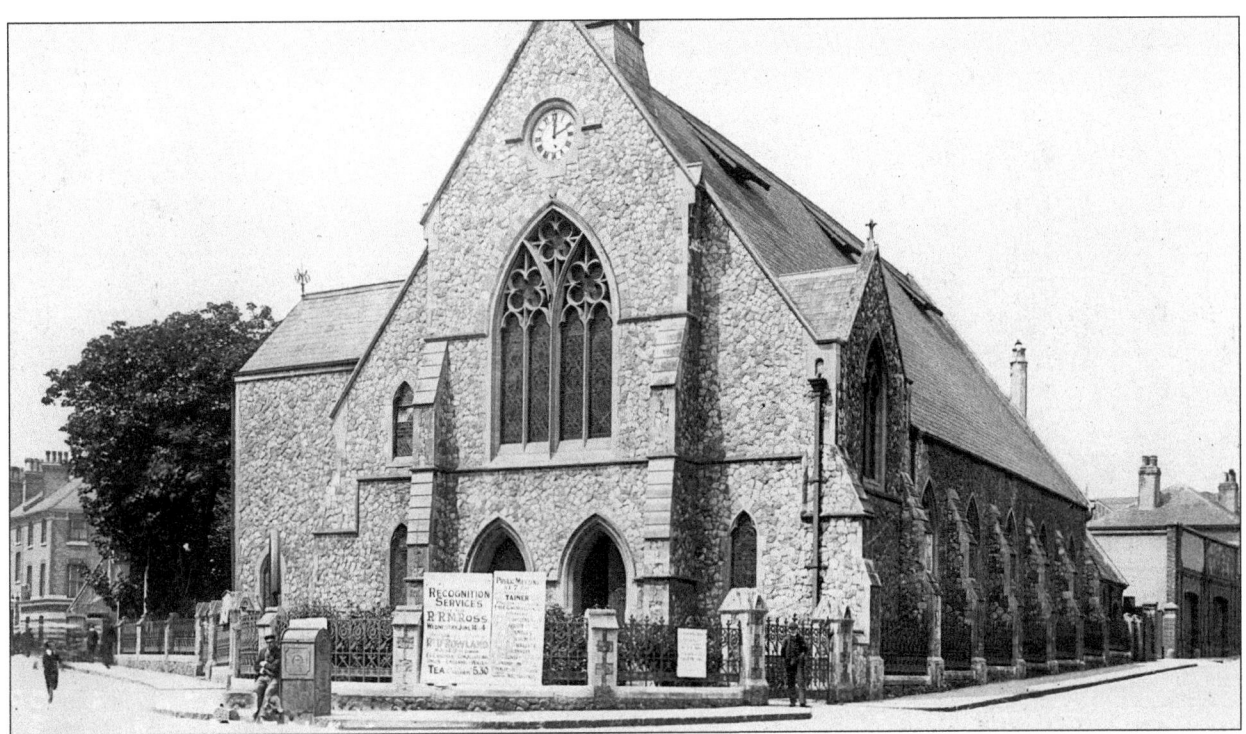

In 1796 the Congregationalists broke away from the Folkestone Anabaptists, from whom they had developed. In 1856 they built this church at the top of Tontine Street. It originally had a spire, but it was removed as its weight was causing subsidence due to the Pent stream passing several feet beneath the foundations. The *Folkestone Chronicle* reported: 'The New Congregational Chapel will open Tuesday 18 August 1857, designed by Mr Messenger, is calculated to seat exclusive of the side galleries 600 persons. The cost will be upwards of £2,000.'

The church and site were put up for sale in c.1973 and advertised as a freehold office site and applications were invited by Smith-Woolley and Perry, chartered surveyors. The London and South East Demolition Contractors demolished the premises in March 1974. This complex of offices named Tontine House, was built on the site and was first occupied by Euro Tunnel, when they moved out the property was sold to Benhams, the first-day cover specialists, and the name changed to Benham House.

Saint Michael and All Angels, Dover Road c.1910. St Michael's was erected in 1873-4 to designs by F. Bodley. The Revd Matthew Woodward laid the foundation stone on 17 April 1873; the church was built of red brick in the Flamboyant style and had a tower with spire, containing eight tubular bells. It opened in 1874 and was consecrated in 1875. One of its longest serving incumbents was the Revd Edward Husband (1873-1908). It replaced a temporary wooden church, known as the Red Barn, which had opened in 1865.

St Michael's Church was closed during World War Two and it remained closed until 1954, when, it was subsequently demolished. This complex of sheltered accommodation, the Sherwood Trust Homes were built on the site with monies from the Sherwood Trust.

The Congregational Mission Hall & School, Canterbury Road, was designed by Joseph Gardner the architect, and built in red, with Bath stone dressings by the local builder Jenners at a cost of £3,000. The hall was 60ft by 23ft each side, it had four rooms with revolving shutters so when the hall was required for meetings and large gatherings these shutters were raised to provide space for 700 people. The foundation stone was laid on Wednesday 13 July 1892 and opened on Wednesday 12 July 1893. The town rapidly expanding to the north caused the need for the church.

The Congregational Mission Hall & School, Canterbury Road, was demolished in 1971 the site is now occupied by this complex of flats Talford Court.

The Wesleyan Methodist Church at the junction of Grace Hill and Dover Road. Folkestone Wesleyan Methodists formed a group in 1824, meeting in a room in Elgar's Yard. They had a small chapel in the old High Street in 1831 and built another in Sandgate Road next to the King's Arms in 1852. It was decided that Folkestone would be the headquarters of the circuit and so in 1864 they began to build this church. It was built of stone in Early English style with a tower surmounted by a graceful spire. The church opened on 31 March 1866.

The Methodist Church was demolished by the London and South Coast Demolition Contractors in March and April 1976. Today the site is occupied by Grace Court, which was built in 1987. It is a development of 26 one-bedroom sheltered flats for up to 33 people. There are 19 flats for single people and seven flats for couples.

The Baptist Church in Rendezvous Street. During the difficult economic days of the 1820s plans were started to replace the Mill Bay Church with the first Rendezvous Street Church. It was built in 1845 on the site of cowsheds and stables at a cost of £2,000. Within a few years the church proved to be too small and under the direction of Revd William Sampson, who was minister from 1867, this present church was built in the Italian style, but the ornamentation of the façade is Corinthian, it seated 900 people and opened on 4 August 1874.

Due to the spiralling cost of maintaining the Baptist church it was sold in 1989 and the Baptists moved to brand new premises in Hill Road. Their old church in Rendezvous Street was converted into the Baptist Galleries, which consisted of 28 shop units created in Victorian style, set on two floors around a central restaurant. The Baptist Galleries did not succeed and in March 1994 the Council passed plans for it to be used as a Theatre. After the Imagination Theatre School moved out the building was converted into a pub as seen here under the name of Wetherspoons, which opened in May 1998.

The Emmanuel Proprietary Church in Cheriton Road was built in 1882 it was a plain brick building and was erected under a trust deed which, during the lease, provided services of a strictly Evangelical character. The last incumbent was Revd A.E. Glover MA.

The Emmanuel Church closed in 1911 and the premises were used by Goodall's, School of Physical Culture. Mr Robert Henry Goodall was an instructor in calisthenics, fencing, and all kinds of Swedish exercises. By 1915 the school had closed and Rowland-Rouse Ltd, motor engineers, occupied the premises. Walter's furniture dealers last occupied the shop before being demolished in 1973 to make way for a new road. The Emmanuel Church stood where the centre reservation is today. The building in the photograph is the Catholic church.

CHURCHES AND CHAPELS

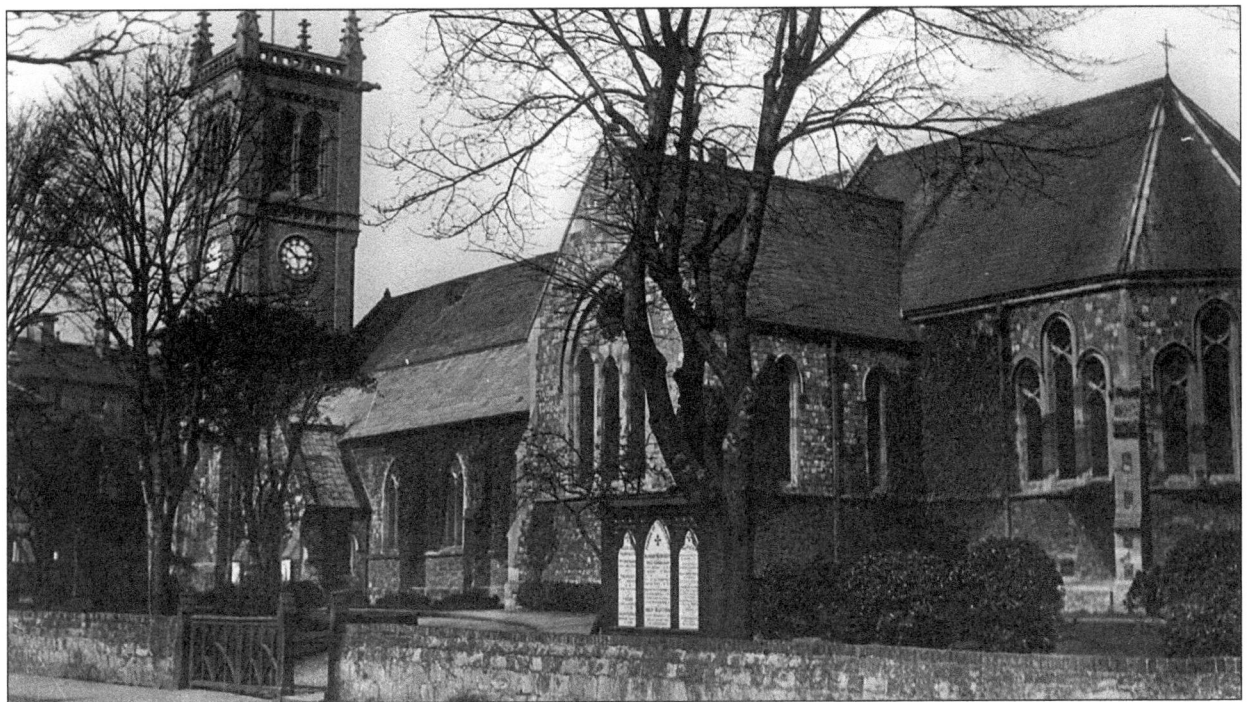

Christ Church, Sandgate Road, was designed by Sidney Smurke and built on land donated by Lord Radnor also the sole cost was defrayed by him. It was built of Kentish ragstone with Bath stone dressings, in a plain Gothic style, and had a tower containing one bell. The Christ Church was consecrated on 27 July 1850 and was an ecclesiastical parish, formed in 1851.

On Sunday morning, 17 May 1942, enemy attacks destroyed Christ Church killing two local women, Vera Emily Ansell and Harriet May Thompson. This present-day photograph, taken on Tuesday 6 November 2001, shows the Clock Tower which survived the bombing and the grounds laid out as a garden of remembrance for the troops that lost their lives during conflicts.

Hotels and Public Houses

THE King's Arms was one of Folkestone's first hotels, it opened in 1692 in Shellons Lane (Guildhall Street) by the site of the present Town Hall, but between 1782 and 1792 it moved to the corner of Sandgate Road. In 1834 a new frontage was built, by which time it was an important staging post for coaches and was one of Folkestone's premier hotels.

After the coming of the railway in 1843 and the increase in visitors, a decision to develop the town was made by Lord Radnor in 1849. The town had started to become a popular and fashionable seaside resort, consequently many hotels were built. One of the first was the Pavilion Hotel, designed by William Cubitt and built by the South-Eastern Railway Company in 1843. Many more were to follow including Bates Hotel in Sandgate Road (1859), later renamed the Esplanade, the West Cliff Hotel (1857) – which was later called the Majestic Hotel, Queen's Hotel in Sandgate Road (1884), Wampach Hotel on Castle Hill Avenue (1886), Hundert's Hotel in Bouverie Road West (1892) – later renamed Princes Hotel, The Metropole Hotel (1897), Grand Mansions (1903) – later to be renamed the Grand Hotel and The Lyndhurst Hotel in Sandgate Road (1918). By 1865 there was also 151 lodging houses in the town.

In 1928 the Rose Hotel was acquired by Montague Burton & Co to build a men's out-fitters; the hotel was subsequently demolished.

After the two world wars, the increase in car ownership and the popularity of continental holidays, Folkestone catered for day-trippers, language students and short-break visitors, consequently many of the hotels and boarding houses were either converted into flats or demolished.

The Queen's Hotel was demolished in 1963 to build a shop and offices.

The Majestic Hotel was demolished in 1964 the site is now occupied by a complex of shops and offices.

The Esplanade Hotel was demolished in 1972 to build a complex of shops and offices.

The Wampach Hotel was demolished in 1975 to build a block of flats.

The Prince's Hotel was demolished in 1976 the site is now part of the police station gardens.

Mr Burstin acquired the Royal Pavilion Hotel in 1960. The hotel was demolished in 1981-2 to build a 481-bedroom motel. The current owners of the Burstin Hotel, the Grand Hotel Group, specialise in short breaks that include a variety of entertainments and a day trip to France by Seacat. The hotel is a boon to the town.

The Lyndhurst Hotel was acquired by McCarthy and Stone Ltd. in 1983 and was demolished to build a complex of flats called Home Pine House.

The Pavilion Hotel (right of picture) was designed by William Cubitt and built by the South-Eastern Railway Company. Building commenced in 1843 to coincide with the coming of the railway. The other building in the photograph, Harbour House, was also built in 1843 for the directors and officers of the South-Eastern Railway and included the Harbour Master's residence.

The Royal Pavilion Hotel was enlarged in 1845 and again in 1850. The harbour company's office, or Clock House Building as it was locally known, was demolished in 1899 to make way for further extensions to the Royal Pavilion Hotel at which time a new red brick façade was built with terracotta window and door reveals as seen in the picture.

The Royal Pavilion Hotel was requisitioned during World War Two and was released in December 1954, remaining empty until the premises were purchased by Mr Burstin, a councillor from Southend-on-Sea. He converted them into flats for the elderly, the first of which was occupied in September 1960. Mr Burstin demolished the Royal Pavilion Hotel in 1981-2 to make way for this building, the Burstin Motel, to be managed by his son Ivor. The Burstin Motel was sold in 1988 to Land Leisure Plc. when it became the Hotel Burstin, the premises have changed hands a number of times since and in 2000 it was taken over by the Grand Hotel Group and is now known as the Grand Burstin.

The True Briton Hotel in Harbour Street, formerly the Cock, started in business c.1741; by 1792 the premises are listed as the True Briton. The man standing by the doorway is Gladstone Martin the landlord from 1926 to 1943. The pub was closed between 1943 and 1946 due to damage by a shell on 2 March 1943, after which Gladstone's son, David, took over the business. He was there until 1959 when he moved to the Eagle Tavern.

Due to the decline in trade at the True Briton the brewers Whitbread decided to incorporate the house

with the joining Old Harbour Crab and Oyster House (formerly the Harbour Inn). This is when the building lost its charming glazed tile façade. In 1990 the name of the combined pubs was changed back from the Old Crab and Oyster House to the Harbour Inn.

The Royal George, 18 Beach Street, formerly known as the Mermaid, c.1717 up to the present day. By 1734 it appears the premises were trading under the name Royal George. The hotel was severely damaged in World War Two by a parachute mine, on 18 November 1940, rendering the hotel's top three floors beyond repair. However, after the top three floors were demolished, the Royal George continued trading as a public house.

It was not until 1958 that Fremlins restored the building after which it continued trading until the early 1980s when Whitbread, who held the house since their amalgamation with Fremlins, closed it. In 1984 local businessman Jimmy Godden purchased the premises and completely rebuilt the building as can be seen in the photograph.

The Dover Castle temperance and commercial hotel, 95 Dover Street; the proprietor was George James Foster from between 1882-7 until 1895 when the business was taken over by R. Foster and then George Jonathan Foster respectively. It appears that the name Dover was dropped about 1905 and the name was as seen in the photograph. The family ran the business until shells destroyed the premises on 5 July 1943.

Today the site of the Castle Hotel is occupied by a detached house (next to Russell & Wheeler) and a terrace of maisonettes, part of which can be seen here on the right of the photograph. Both were built about 1955.

HOTELS AND PUBLIC HOUSES

The Railway Tavern, 119 Dover Road, was in business from c.1863 to 1971. Thomas Southall seen in the picture was the proprietor from 1899 to 1926. The Railway Tavern had a very attractive glazed tile ground floor façade with leaded-light windows.

Due to the decline in trade the brewers Whitbread decided to close the Railway Tavern in 1971 and sell for redevelopment. The premises remained empty until they were demolished with two shops in 1973 to make way for this complex of eight flats named Abbott's Court, costing £209,000.

The Rose Hotel, 24 Rendezvous Street, was in business from c.1717 to 1928. The Rose was one of Folkestone's old coaching inns whose fortunes began to decline following the arrival of the railway in 1843. The Rose Hotel was sold in 1928 to Burtons the tailors and the licence was transferred to the Leas Cliff Hall. Burtons demolished the Rose in January-February 1928 to build a new store.

Sixty-one years later in 1989 the former Burton's shop became licensed once again under the name of Muswells Café Bar. In 1995 it became an Irish theme pub called Scruffy Murphys, which closed on 22 March 2000. Fitzpatricks Café-Bar-Bistro and Restaurant from 20 April 2000 occupied the premises up until 22 August 2000. Today the Zoo occupies the premises as seen in the picture.

Opposite page, top: The King's Arms Hotel, 2 Sandgate Road, was one of Folkestone's first hotels it opened in 1692 in Shellons Lane (Guildhall Street) by the site of the present old Town Hall, but between 1782 and 1792 it moved to its present site on the corner of Sandgate Road. In 1843 a new frontage was built, by which time it was an important staging post for coaches. The King's Arms closed on Sunday 18 December 1881. The building on the left belongs to Michael Valyer, fly and omnibus proprietor.

Opposite page, bottom: The demolition of the King's Arms started on 24 June 1882 to make way for the Queen's Hotel, which opened 18 January 1885, costing £30,000 to build. During the hotel's life, the Bodega bar and long bar were both popular to locals and holidaymakers alike.

HOTELS AND PUBLIC HOUSES

Demolition work started on the Queen's Hotel in January 1963, taking three months to complete. Queen's House was built on the site, Burtons the tailors occupied the ground floor shop and the offices above are occupied by Kent County Council Social Services. The shop is now occupied by Bonmarchè clothing store.

The Esplanade Hotel, formerly Bates Hotel, 49-55 Sandgate Road. The hotel had a number of proprietors down the years and in 1919 it was taken over by Mr W. Rosenz and this is when the name was changed to Esplanade. The hotel was sold for redevelopment and demolished in 1973.

A complex of four shops now occupies the site of the Esplanade Hotel. In December 2001 they were occupied by; Stead and Simpson's shoe shop, Dixons, Claire's jewellery, and the National Westminster Bank.

The Bristol Hotel, The Leas. Mrs Frank Funnell established the hotel at 2-3 The Leas in 1931. In 1938 the business was taken over by Mr & Mrs E.F. Kennett, who in 1939 expanded the business by occupying number four. In 1947 numbers three and four are listed as a private hotel the proprietor being A. Ward, and in 1949 numbers three and four are listed as the Bristol Hotel (proprietor P.J. Newman). The premises were demolished for redevelopment in 1968.

The Bristol and Wythenshawe Hotels closed in 1967 and were subsequently demolished in 1968 for redevelopment. Today the sites are occupied by the Bikash Tandoori Indian restaurant, a tall complex of flats called number one The Leas (formerly Fortune House of the Welfare Insurance Company) and a complex of maisonettes called Priors Leas.

Moore's Hotel; 11, 12 and 13 The Leas. John Wright Moore started the business with a boarding house at No11 The Leas between 1883 and 1887. In 1906 he took No 12 and in 1910 Nos 11 and 12 are listed as Pension and Private Hotel. In 1914 the hotel expanded once more by adding No13 and in 1921 the proprietor was Muriel Moore. Mrs F. Saxby was the last proprietress when the hotel closed in about 1960.

Moore's hotel has been replaced with this complex of flats and maisonettes called Whitcliffs. The development started in 1970 with Mr Gerald Glover, owner of the Metropole Hotel, at the helm. 38 flats and 18 maisonettes with underground parking were built on the site by the local builder Jenner & Son Ltd at a cost of £350,000.

The West Cliff Hotel, 138 Sandgate Road. On 27 June 1857, the *Folkestone Chronicle* reported that four large houses known as Langhorne-Gardens were being converted into a hotel to be called the West Cliff Hotel, the owner being Mr T. Masters from London. In 1898 the hotel underwent extensive alterations and was the first customer of the newly formed Folkestone Electricity Supply Company. During World War One the hotel was used as a Canadian Army ear and eye hospital.

Immediately after World War One the West Cliff Hotel had its name changed to Majestic as seen in the picture. The Majestic closed in 1962 and was subsequently demolished two years later after which the site was used as a temporary car park until 1970.

In 1970 Mr Gerald Glover, managing director of Edger Investments Ltd, started the Majestic House development. It consisted of 4,000 square feet of office space, seven shop units and seven maisonettes built on 1.76 acres, which is bounded by Sandgate Road, Castle Hill Avenue and Bouverie Road West. The main contractors were Sir Robert McAlpine & Sons Ltd. The present-day picture shows the complex of shops and maisonettes in Sandgate Road called Majestic Parade.

The Lyndhurst Hotel, 12-15 Clifton Gardens. The name Lyndhurst started at 13 Clifton Gardens which was a lodging house. By 1913, Nos 12, 13 and 14 were listed as Lyndhurst private suites with electric lift. After World War One the premises at 12-15 Clifton Gardens became the Lyndhurst Hotel.

The Lyndhurst Hotel was sold for redevelopment, planning permission to build 138 private sheltered flats for the elderly was granted in September 1982 to the developers McCarthy and Stone Ltd, of New Milton, Hampshire. The Lyndhurst was demolished to make way for this complex of flats built in 1983-4 and is called Home Pine House.

The Princes Hotel, 44 Bouverie Road West, formerly Hundert's Private Hotel was renamed the Regina Hotel c1920 and was run by Max Wilhelm Hundert from 1892 to 1931. In 1933 the premises were taken over by Princes Mansions Ltd, and the hotel was renamed the Princes Hotel.

The Princes Hotel closed in April 1976 and was demolished in August the same year and the site was used to extend the Orion Insurance Company's gardens (now Folkestone police station).

The Wampach Hotel, 31-37 Castle Hill Avenue, opened in 1886 and was named after its proprietor Charles Constant Wampach who came to England from Diekirch, Luxembourg in 1875. The hotel in its hey-day was one of the most luxurious in Folkestone, patronised by the nobility and gentry and due to the steady increase of visitors the premises had been enlarged four times by 1900. The hotel was completely refurbished, after being occupied by troops during World War Two and it eventually reopened in 1950. In 1952 Mr Harry Sargent became the hotel's manager and later became the owner.

The Hotel Continental Wampach (as it was later known) closed in 1973 but due to a number of sales falling through and the rejection of planning permission the building stood empty. In 1974 the building was wrecked by fire and it was partially demolished the following year, but demolition was not completed until 1983. Planning permission was granted to Wimpey to build 51 sheltered flats, with a warden's home and communal facilities. Building work started in 1985 and the first residents moved in during December 1986.

Streets and Trades

IN THE 1820s Folkestone's main shopping streets were: Gulstone Street (South Street), King's Bridge Street (Beach Street), Pent Buildings, Old Seagate, Brook Street (Harbour Way) and the High Street.

After the coming of the railway in 1843, Folkestone started to attract more visitors, so in 1849 Lord Radnor appointed a London architect, Mr Sydney Smirke, to oversee the development the town.

One proposal was to build a shopping centre in the Pent Valley area so a Folkestone Tontine Building Company was formed with the intention of making a road up the valley to meet Mill Lane (Dover Road), the stream being confined within a culvert under the road. The new road was begun in 1848 and it was intended to provide a modern shopping centre in the Regency style. Unfortunately the town was not ready for this development and only the lower half of the street was built at first. But by the 1890s Tontine Street, as it was named, became the busiest shopping centre in the town.

The next step in the development came in 1855, when the council obtained an Act to extend the limits of the Borough of Folkestone, which enabled the Corporation to make new streets and other improvements like paving, lighting and draining. In the Harbour area dwellings bordering the lower stretch of the Pent stream were demolished to build Harbour Street. Tontine Street was extended to meet Mill Lane, which was renamed Dover Road. Rendezvous Street, formerly Butcher Row, was widened to 40ft. Grigg's Lane, which ran from the Shakespeare Hotel down to Copthall Gardens, was built up and renamed Shellons Street. By the mid-1850s, Sandgate Road was gradually built up as far as Christ Church, and the side roads were opened such as West Cliff Gardens, West Terrace and Bouverie Place leading to Bouverie Square. By 1865 a few houses appeared in Victoria Grove, Shellons Street, Dover Road above St Michael's Church and in London Street. By 1874 the Wear Bay Estate started to be developed with a few dwellings built at East Cliff, Waterloo Terrace and Trafalgar Terrace. Houses also appeared along Broadmead Lane, at the junction of Cheriton Road and Bouverie Road East, and in the upper stretch of Dover Road. The development of Foord Road and Canterbury Road started in 1866. A new shopping centre started to develop in the lower end of Sandgate Road and had reached Bouverie Place by 1900. The development of Penfold Road by the Council in 1896 provided much needed houses. In 1931 Bobby's department store moved from Rendezvous Street to purpose built premises in Sandgate Road, they were followed by the Penny Bazaar (forerunner of Marks & Spencer), who moved from the High Street to Sandgate Road. The Council developed Hill Road and Wood Avenue in the early 1920s followed by the private development of Joyes Road in 1929.

In 1935 the old houses in Radnor Street, East Street, Bates Alley, Dunn's Alley and Clouts Alley were demolished and replaced with new houses for the fishermen. Work started on the Crete Way Down council estate in the early 1950s.

The Harbour Street and Beach Street areas were destroyed during World War Two, prompting more businesses to move into Sandgate Road, so the town continued its Westward drift towards Manor Road. With the introduction of supermarkets many small traders went out of business and their corner shops were converted into living accommodation. The town's 18-hole golf course was sold for development in about 1969 and the Lynwood estate was built.

In 1972-3 Shellons Street, the lower end of Cheriton Road, Bouverie Road East and the north-west side of Bouverie Square, were demolished to make way for a new road. The Bouverie Square site is now occupied by a multi-story car park and a tower block of offices occupied by Saga. Sandgate Road and Guildhall Street became pedestrianised in 1984, establishing the area as the main shopping centre. Present day Tontine Street is mainly occupied with cafés, restaurants, take-away restaurants, amusement arcades and nightclubs.

The shops in the Old High Street are currently occupied by cafés, souvenir shops, gift shops, antique shops, a stamp and collectors shop, a homemade sweet shop and a baker.

At the present time the north-east side of Bouverie Square, the south-east side of Middleburg Square and the south-west side of Alexandra Gardens, are being demolished for a future development, a new town centre shopping complex.

The building on the left of the London and Paris Hotel was built as the County Skating Rink, on the site of an old anchor yard (a place where the sailing ships could purchase an anchor). Mr Robert Forsythe opened the County Skating Rink in Lower Sandgate Road in 1911. Mr H. E. Savery converted it into the Harbour Garage as seen here in 1920. The name changed to Auto Pilot's in 1930.

Auto Pilot's Garage was demolished in April 1971 and a filling station was built on the site. The filling station was demolished in 2001 and this car park was built in its place. It is interesting to note that the name of the London and Paris also changed in that year to Gillespie's.

STREETS AND TRADES

South Street: formerly Gulston Street looking towards the High Street. To the left can be seen part of the Princess Royal public house, first licensed in 1845 and on the right is the London and Paris Hotel first licensed in 1853. Note the sign, 'Café Boulogne'. It had at one time been a public house called The Victoria, between 1839 and 1905. Further down the street there is a maze of small shops.

The buildings in South Street apart from the London and Paris, Princess Royal, True Briton and Harbour Inn, were demolished in 1952. The area was then laid out in gardens and a shelter was erected in 1959. The harbour-side facelift of 2001 saw the shelter demolished, the flowerbeds redesigned, and the whole area repaved as seen in the picture.

Harbour Street just after the turn of the century (1900). The buildings to the left backed on to South Street, giving them front and back access. All these buildings apart from the one in the centre far distance were either severely damaged or destroyed by a parachute mine on 18 November 1940.

Most of the buildings in Harbour Street and the surrounding area were cleared away in the 1950s to make provision for tree planting, shrubberies, flowerbeds and a car park. Last year saw the whole area improved by the harbour-side facelift project costing £1.3 million, part of which can be seen in this present-day picture.

The Old High Street is a narrow cobblestone street running from Harbour Street to Rendezvous Street. In earlier times it was the main thoroughfare to the Bayle and Rendezvous Street as shown on Powell's Survey of 1782. It was also one of the town's main retail shopping streets up until the 1930s.

The cobblestoned Old High Street, with its mixture of dwellings and shops, survives today. It is a reminder of Folkestone's history and is one of the town's oldest thoroughfares. There are not many family retail shops left in the Old High Street today. Most of them have been put out of business by supermarkets and the town's continual drift westwards. Most of the premises here, which are occupied, sell gifts and souvenirs.

Mr Ernest Edgar Wakeling, tobacconist, 77 Old High Street. Mr Wakeling's fine window display consists of confectionery in the left-hand window and tobacco in the right, his shop is typical of the 1930s when someone could buy their tobacco by the ounce whether it was for chewing, smoking in a pipe or rolling cigarettes.

Mr Wakeling's shop, at 77 Old High Street, is now part of an amusement arcade owned by the entrepreneur Jimmy Godden.

North Street formerly New Island, commenced building sometime after 1698 in the style of 17th-century terrace houses in Yarmouth. This photograph was taken in 1947 when most of the properties were not inhabited because of damage they sustained during World War Two. The Commissioners of Paving made some of the street name changes, including this one, in August 1796.

Most of the old buildings in North Street were demolished in 1952 and this complex of flats was built on the right-hand side, while the Folkestone yacht and motorboat club headquarters are on the left, just out of the picture.

Radnor Street, formerly Fishermen's Row, looking towards the east in 1928. The first building on the right is Whittingstall's General Stores, the building with the chequered brickwork is the Radnor Lodging House, formerly Radnor Inn 1843-76. Further to its right the first of the two projecting signs is the Jubilee and the second is the Oddfellows' Arms.

On 4 October 1933, under the Housing Acts of 1925 and 1930, the Council passed a resolution declaring the area to be cleared of its slums. Radnor Street was earmarked as one of the streets to have some of its premises demolished which took place in 1935. The picture shows how the right side of Radnor Street looks today.

The left-hand side of Radnor Street looking east in 1928; the junction with North Street can be seen on the left. All the properties the eye can see were demolished in 1935. Here are some of the names of people who had their properties compulsorily purchased: Emily Minter, Jane Elliott, Richard Godden Sanders, Ernest Nicholls, Iris Everall Court, Louisa Florence Sanders, George Major, Domenico Flessati, Alfred May, George Beer and Rigden Ltd, and Charles Winter Garrett and Henry Charles Manning Sisk the Trustees of Joseph Johnson deceased.

The left-hand side of Radnor Street looking east and the junction of North Street on the left, as it looks today. On the extreme left can be seen part of the North Street flats built in 1952, while the houses and the Front public house, formerly the Oddfellows, were built after the slum clearance in the mid-1930s.

The east end of Radnor Street looking eastwards in 1935. On the left the lady standing in the doorway is Mrs Ethel Lee, while further along the road the houses are being demolished. The two protruding signs on the right belong to the Jubilee Inn and Oddfellows Arms respectively. In the far distance can be seen the new Jubilee public house followed by the new fishermen's houses.

East Street, formerly Radnor Street, as viewed today, looking east. On the left can be seen the fishermen's stores, while on the right are the backs of the houses on the Stade. The large building at the end of the road is the Mariner's public house, formerly the Jubilee, which was, renamed Carpenters in 1988.

The Stade and East Street: looking north-west in c.1924. The large brick building on the right was the South-Eastern and Chatham Railway Company's Marine Workshops, which closed in 1922; the building was later converted into bathing cabins. The old fishermen's houses to the left are in East Street.

On the right is part of a complex of flats called Harbour Point, which was built in 1988 on the site of the Sunny Sands restaurant, formerly the site of the South-Eastern and Chatham Railway Company's Marine Workshops. To the left of the flats are the fishermen's houses built in 1935, on the Stade, formerly a part of East Street.

Wear Bay Road looking north-east into Wear Bay Crescent in about 1911. It is interesting to note that the east side of Wear Bay Crescent has not yet been developed and one can see Martello Tower number one. The Ecclesbourne Boarding house at Nos 16 and 17 are the last properties in Wear Bay Road; the properties following them are in Wear Bay Crescent.

The present-day view of Wear Bay Road, looking into Wear Bay Crescent, does not allow you to see Martello number one, the houses on the east side of Wear Bay Crescent, most of which were built in 1929-30, block the view.

The Bruce-Porter Hospital home (Dr Barnardo's), 9-11 Wear Bay Crescent, on the corner of Segrave Road. The home opened in 1920 and remained until 1964.

This complex of sheltered flats called St Clement's Court, opened by the Queen Mother in 1974, now occupies the site of the Bruce-Porter Hospital, 9-11 Wear Bay Crescent.

Mrs Ovenden's confectionery shop on the corner of Warren Road and Thanet Gardens 1908-10. The premises seen here appear to have been converted into a general shop about 1900, the first proprietor being R.E. Cladingbowl.

No 40 Warren Road on the corner of Thanet Gardens ceased being a shop in 1984. The premises as seen here were converted back into living accommodation. Another example of the times we live in where these small traders cannot compete with the supermarket chains.

Dover Street (Harbour Way) looking south from the junction of Radnor Bridge Road in 1938. A shell destroyed the properties along from Stokes Bros, coal merchants, down to Fosters Castle Hotel on 5 July 1943.

Harbour Way, formerly Dover Street (the name was changed in 1956), looking south from the junction of Radnor Bridge Road. The properties destroyed by shellfire, as seen in the last picture, were replaced in 1955 with one detached house (next to the Russell and Wheeler sign) followed by four maisonettes as seen in the picture.

Robert Martin ran this general shop at 42 Dover Street from 1888 to 1890 when it was taken over by Mrs Harriot Martin seen here in the doorway. Mrs Martin ran the business from 1890 to 1913 when it was taken over by a C.D. Boulter.

The Blessing of the Fisheries procession making its way down Dover Street from St Peters Church to the fishmarket in 1938. It is interesting to note that the procession passes by the newsagents and tobacconists shop belonging to A.J. Bliss, at 44 Dover Street, the family ran the business from 1927 until the mid-1940s.

Demolition work in progress at Harbour Way (Dover Street) on the 28 February 1959. The two shops seen in the previous pictures of Dover Street stood next to these two remaining houses. The nearest of the two houses belonged to Mr Harry Sharp it was compulsory purchased by the Council for £80.

The present-day photograph of Harbour Way shows a complex of flats, which were built by the Council in the gardens of the old Dover Street premises. The part of a building seen on the left is Kingsbridge Court, which spans Harbour Way at the junction of Harvey Street.

Dover Street just above the junction of Little Fenchurch Street on 27 July 1927. It is interesting to note how narrow the street is, just wide enough for the Morris Commercial van which is coming down the road. The cycle business of W.R. Wicks can be seen on the right.

Dover Street was severely damaged during World War Two and the street was designated for redevelopment. The properties were compulsory purchased by the Council and work started in 1955 by widening the road and changing the name to Harbour Way. Two terraces of houses comprising of 15 properties were built between St Michael's Street and Harvey Street, followed by blocks of flats seen in the picture.

STREETS AND TRADES

Great Fenchurch Street looking up into Little Fenchurch Street. On the left is the turning into Bennett's Yard, followed by the junction of Little Fenchurch Street. The photograph was taken in 1937 when some properties were being demolished during a slum clearance. The sign in Little Fenchurch Street belongs to the George III public house.

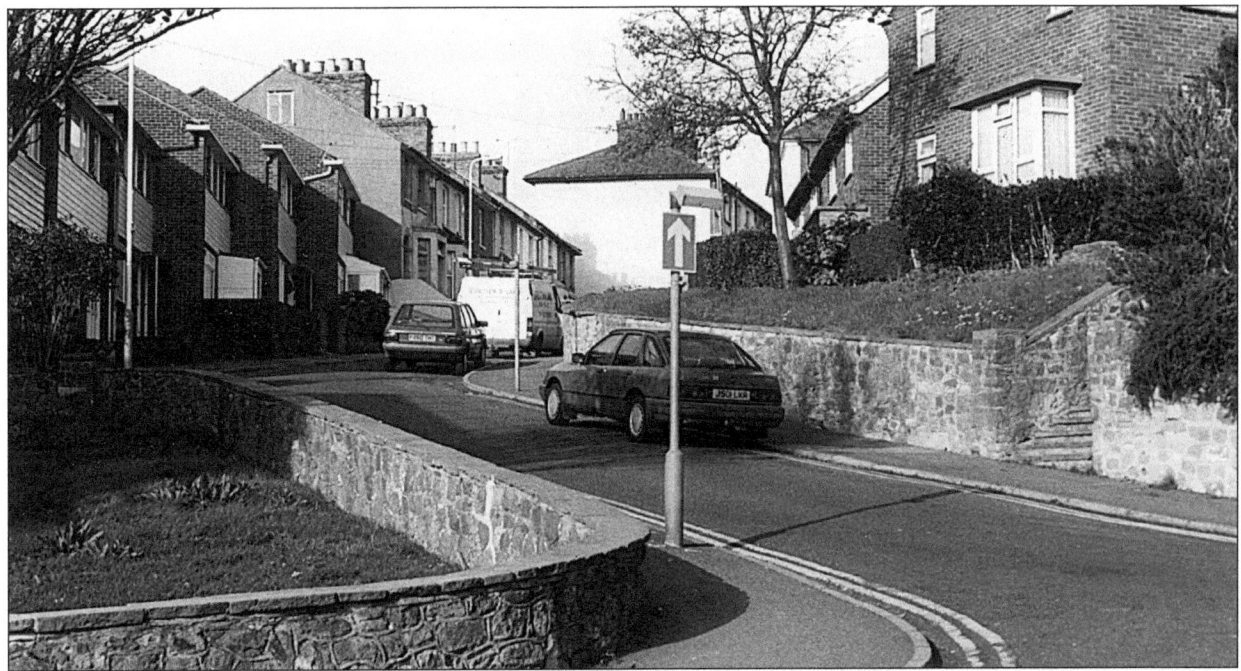

Looking up St Michael's Street from the junction of Harbour Way. After the redevelopment Little Fenchurch Street became part of St Michael's Street in 1961-2. The George III public house closed in 1961 and the site today is occupied by five town houses built in 1963, as seen here on the left.

Seagate Street at the junction of Dover Street in 1936-7. Mr Henry Warren boot warehouse, 1 Seagate Street, was in business at these premises from 1902 to 1936.

A parachute mine destroyed the properties in Seagate Street on 18 November 1940. Seagate Street became part of Harbour Way during the redevelopment of the 1950s. Today Mr Warren's shop would have stood where the tree stands above the bend in the rock wall at the road junction.

Looking up Tontine Street in about 1903. A Folkestone Tontine Building Company was formed with the intention of making a road up the Valley to meet Mill Lane (Dover Road), the Pent stream being confined within a culvert under the road. The new road began in 1848 and it was intended to provide a modern shopping centre in the Regency style. The town was not ready for this development and only the lower half of the street was built at first. But by the 1890s Tontine Street, as it was named, became the busiest shopping centre in the town.

Looking up Tontine Street today you find it is not the busy shopping centre it once was. The town has steadily drifted further west along the Sandgate Road leaving Tontine Street with hardly any retail trade. The street has a combination of cafés, restaurants, takeaways, amusement arcades and nightclubs. It is interesting to note that on the left-hand side of the street you can distinctly see where the Regency style building stopped.

Foord Road looking north-west in the early 1900s. Five arches of the 19 arch railway viaduct built in 1843, can be seen in the picture. Note the two little boys pulling a handcart loaded with bushel baskets, while two young girls try to cross the road.

Plans to compulsory purchase 43 houses and one newsagent's shop in Foord Road was proposed by the Council in August 1973. The Council plans eventually got the go-ahead and properties this side of the viaduct were demolished in 1980-1. They have been replaced with 49 sheltered flats and 22 maisonettes as seen in the picture.

The Foord Valley in about 1857 a few years before Bradstone Road and Foord Lane were opened. The railway viaduct was designed by William Cubitt and built in 1843 to span the Foord Valley. The large house in the centre is the home of the owner of Bradstone Mill. The open area to the left of the house was used as a ropewalk. On the left is Bulldog Lane leading past Bradstone Mill. The lamp and brick wall mark the position of the culvert, which the Pent stream goes under.

This present-day picture is looking up Bradstone Road from the junction of Dover Road. Bradstone Road took its name from the Bradstone Water Mill, which was run by the Stace family from about 1720 for well over a hundred years. The whole area has been completely transformed since the earlier picture.

Bradstone Road at the junction of Dover Road. The building at the junction of Dover Road was formerly a tanner's; L.F. & W. Jordan, tobacconist and confectioners last occupied the shop and it was demolished in 1972. The Folkestone Co-operative Society occupies the large building behind Jordan's at 28-34 Dover Road. They started at 28 Dover Road in 1892, expanding to No 34 in 1923 when the new façade was built.

After the premises occupied by S. Lummus & Jordan's were demolished, the site was not developed until 1996 when the New Health Centre was built, seen here on the left. The Folkestone Co-operative closed in 1972 and the New Generation Bingo hall now occupies part of the ground floor while the rest of the building remains empty.

Alfred Olby's wholesale ironmongers at, 21-23 Dover Road, formerly Ramell's the coachbuilders. Olby's were at these premises from 1926 to about 1980 when they were taken over by Graham Ford, later becoming Graham's builders merchants.

Graham's builders merchants at 21-23 Dover road was demolished in the second half of 1994. The site along with the undeveloped plot on the corner of Bradstone Road and the site that was formerly Vale's Yard, are now occupied by this new health centre. Costing £2 million, the health centre was opened by the Kent Community Healthcare NHS Trust in January 1996.

The funeral of Police Constable Henry William Scott assembles outside his house at 35 Peter Street, on 8 May 1912. Mr Scott had died on 3 May, aged 58.

In 1962 the terrace of houses on the left-hand side of Peter Street seen in the last picture were compulsory purchased by the Council and demolished. This complex of 26 Council flats and garages built in 1967-8 and called Rowen Court now occupy the site.

St Mary's National School, Dover Road, was built on a deed of grant from the Earl of Folkestone for 575 children costing £4,000. It was founded in 1854 by Matthew Woodward vicar of the Parish Church and opened in 1855 with Charles Tye as the master, Mrs Jane A. Tye as the mistress and Miss Esther Elliott appointed infants' mistress. In 1902 the school had an average attendance of 200 junior boys, 200 junior girls and 150 infants. It later became a junior girls school with Arthur Pendlebury-Green as the headmaster.

St Mary's School moved to new premises in Warren Road in June 1982 and the old school in Dover Road was put up for sale for an asking price of about £90,000. Part of the school was used by St Mary's Social Club, now Dover Road Social club and the other part by a playgroup, which is now occupied by the Shepway Amateur Boxing Club. In 1994 the unused part of the school was sold for development and demolished in April and May that year. That part of the site is now occupied by these five town houses called St Mary's Terrace.

Mr J. Franklin, Grocery and Provisions, 103 Dover Road. Mr Franklin's family ran the grocery business from 1901 to 1947. Mr Munday was the proprietor of Munday's fruit and greengrocery business at 105 Dover Road between 1940 and 1947.

The premises of 103 and 105 Dover Road have occupied various family businesses down the years. This present-day picture tells a sad story where family businesses cannot compete with the larger supermarket chains. Shop number 103 has been converted into living accommodation and number 105 into a Private Shop, catering for 'adult' needs. A very sad sign of present-day times!

On the extreme left can be seen the business of W. & R. Fletcher Ltd, butchers, at 105 Dover Road, from 1906 to sometime between 1918-21. Followed by the headquarters of the Cinque Ports Artillery, at 107 Dover Road, who were at these premises from 1867 to 1907. Next is the access to Abbott Road followed by the business of G.I. Willson, wholesale grocer (now occupied by part of Abbott Court).

On the left of this present-day picture can be seen the Private Shop, formerly Fletcher's. The premises of the Cinque Ports Artillery were demolished c.1907 to make way for this complex of four shops.

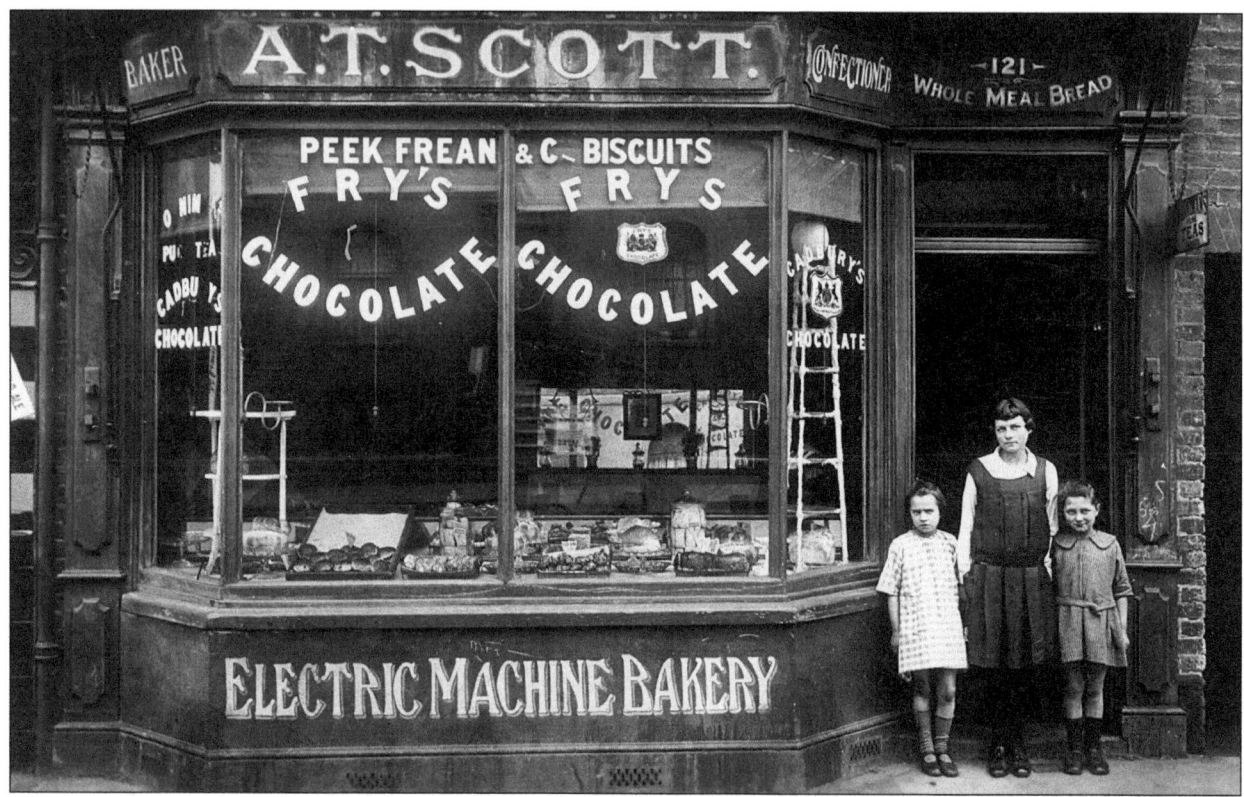

A.T. Scott, baker and confectioner, traded from about 1886 until sometime during World War Two at 121 Dover Road. Note the sign advertising 'Electric Machine Bakery', it must have been state-of-the-art when the photograph was taken.

Tanton Brown Morford, boot and shoe repairer, traded at 121 Dover Road from 1949 up until 1977, when the business was taken over by Fred Heasman who ran the business until retiring through ill health in 1988. The premises are now occupied by, Shupria, Indian Tandoori Takeaway.

Looking up Dover Road, formerly Mill Lane, from Mr Scott's bakery business at 121 Dover Road. It is interesting to note the sign advertising Mr Scott's Electric Machine Bakery is not under the window of this 1904 photograph and that the two premises following Mr Scott's are private houses. The tall Victorian building with the stucco façade is the York Hotel.

The present-day view of Dover Road has not changed that much apart from the absence of the York Hotel. It has been replaced with a terrace of five town houses. The only shop still trading in the same commodity as in the 1904 photograph is a butcher's at 129 Dover Road.

W. Morley, family butcher 129 Dover Road, was in business at this shop from *c.*1899 to 1915. The premises have been occupied by butchers since at least 1885. The shop itself appears to have been built in 1881. It is interesting to note the display of meat outside. The days when this was allowed are long gone. I don't think the environmental health inspector would be very happy if shops were to try this today!

Mr R.J. Burrows the family butcher, 129 Dover Road. Mr Burrows came from Chatham to take this business over on 1 June 1985 from Mr J.B. Lewis who was retiring after running the business since 1962. This butcher's shop is one of only three family butchers left in Folkestone today whereas in 1954 there were 22.

Thomas Freeman, who was hoping to attract railway passengers alighting from the nearby Folkestone Junction Station, opened this building at 139 Dover Road, as the York Hotel in 1845. This was not to be successful and the business failed, after which the premises had rather a chequered life. It became Grove End Preparatory School in 1852, a holiday home for the Union of London Ragged Schools. Then in 1895 it opened as the Grove End Temperance Hotel, after which it reverted back to the York Hotel and in 1918 it was converted into a furniture depository.

After changing hands as a furniture depository, 139 Dover Road was finally demolished in 1968. The site today is occupied by these five town houses.

Looking down Dover Road from the junction of Folly Road *c*.1908. The shop on the left in the foreground is Mr J. Cook's newsagents, while the second protruding sign marks the business of Mrs M. Marsh, 'general carrier, fly, & bus proprietress'. On 6 October 1940, a high-explosive bomb destroyed all the buildings on the left-hand side as far as the first lamp-post.

The present-day photograph, looking down Dover Road from Folly Road, illustrates a number of changes. The premises on the left-hand side, which were destroyed during World War Two, have been replaced with a complex of flats called Rossendale Court and the shop on the right-hand corner of Grove Road has been converted into living accommodation.

STREETS AND TRADES

Dover Road looking up from the Skew Arches in 1905. On the left is Mr F. Ray's boot and shoe shop, followed by Mr A. Huckstepp's tobacconists. Behind the wall and fence on the right-hand side is a row of 13 houses, known as Station Cottages. They were built for railway workers.

The present-day photograph looking up Dover Road from the Skew Arches shows that the two shops on the left foreground have been converted into living accommodation. Again, this is a sign of the times where small traders cannot compete with the supermarket chains.

Canterbury Road looking up from the junction of Wood Avenue in the 1930s. Wood Avenue bus shelter seen here on the right was erected in 1927. On the left-hand side can be seen the farm buildings of Walton Manor Farm. It is interesting to note the number of destinations to where the buses went from this stop: Sandgate, Hythe, Folkestone Harbour, Town Hall and Central Station.

The bus shelter on this present-day photograph, looking up Canterbury Road from the junction of Wood Avenue, is hidden behind bushes. Walton Manor Farm has been replaced with two terraces of town houses and in the distance can be seen part of the Crete Way Down council housing estate built in the early 1950s.

This is Walton Manor Farm House in Canterbury Road. Harold William Snape was the last farmer to run Walton Manor Farm and by 1954 the animals had been disposed of and the farm became a corn merchant's run by Snape & Leslie. The house was last occupied in 1960-1 by Commander Chas S. Britton, RN (ret).

Walton Manor Farm in Canterbury Road was demolished about 1967. The site is now occupied by two terraces of town houses, the first of which was built in 1969.

The New Road as the postcard is captioned ran from Canterbury Road to Cherry Garden Avenue. Lord Radnor made a proposal to build the road under the downs in 1902. The road is in fact an extension of Hill Road laid, out as a dual carriageway before World War One but never made up. The unmade road was a subject of discussion with the Ministry of Transport since before World War Two. As kids in the late 1940s we called it the New Road. It was a safe place for children to cycle and play because there were gates each end to stop it being used by motor vehicles.

The present-day photograph of Churchill Avenue. The New Road (as it was known) is a bypass for traffic from Dover to the M20; Lord Radnor officially opened it on Friday 18 September 1970 and it was built at a cost of £215,000. On the right, two housing estates have been built called Holy Well Avenue and Pilgrim Spring, while on the left one can see the Park Farm Industrial Estate, all of these are post-war developments. It's interesting to note the road is a single carriageway not a dual carriageway as originally laid out.

Caesar's Camp dominates this postcard of Cherry Garden Avenue leading into the unmade Hill Road or the New Road. On the left can be seen Broadmead Farm and Broadmead Manor House, which was built as a farmhouse in 1711.

Cherry Garden Avenue as it looks today. On the left can be seen part of a rock wall that belongs to Broadmead Manor House, which still survives to this day, followed by the junction of Cherry Garden Lane. From this junction the rural scene has given way to housing estates.

Cheriton Road from the junction of Manor Road in about 1875. On the right can be seen the junction of Claremont Road. It's interesting to note that Brockman Road has not been built nor the United Reform Church and that the railway bridge has a brick arch.

Cheriton Road looking towards the Central Station in the present day. The building on the corner of Claremont Road still dominates the picture; it is now a doctor's surgery. The tower of the United Reform Church can just be seen on the left and an iron railway bridge, which opened on 29 June 1893, now spans the Cheriton Road.

The north-west side of Bouverie Square in the 1960s. The building of Bouverie Square commenced in February 1862 and it was one of the major improvements to the town at that time. In the centre of the Bouverie Square there was a large lawn and tennis courts surrounded by trees. This was all swept away in 1955 to build a bus station.

The north-west side of Bouverie Square was demolished in 1972 to make way for the northern distributor road. This block of offices was built in 1977 and called Bouverie House. It stood empty until 1987 when the holiday firm Saga moved in. The north-west side of Bouverie Square is now called Middleburg Square. Sadly, the north-east side of the square is currently being demolished, leaving just the south-west side with Victorian buildings.

Christ Church School at the junction of Cheriton Road and Bouverie Road East. The National Society for the Education of the Poor in the Principles of the Established Church established the National Schools, the first in 1852 being connected with the new Christ Church and known as the Gun School.

Christ Church School was relocated in 1955 to new premises in Brockman Road. The old school became an art centre until being demolished in 1972 to make way for the new Northern Distributor Road. Part of this 575 space multi-storey car park, built by Star (Great Britain) Holdings Limited at a cost of £700,000, is now on the site of Christ Church School.

The south-west side of Cheriton Road: looking towards the Central Station. These five shops stood between Christ Church School and the Bouverie Arms. They were, last occupied by, T.S. Rush (newsagent) Ralph E. Harding (typewriter dealer), Tiara (ladies' hairdressers), Grove Café and Frederick R.D. Hills (butcher).

The five shops in Cheriton Road were demolished in 1972 to make way for the redevelopment of the area. This new road now joins Cheriton road where the five shops stood. On the right can be seen part of the Northfield Nursery School, formerly the Bouverie Arms.

Looking down Cheriton Road from the junction of Bouverie Road East in 1914. This photograph, taken on 26 July 1914, is of the gun carriage funeral of Captain G.H. Talbot. They have just left the Catholic Church and are on their way to the cemetery. It is interesting to note the shop of C. Bull & Son, boot makers & repairs, followed by the Emmanuel Church, the Gun Brewery and Shakespeare Hotel.

The premises mentioned in the previous picture – C. Bull & Son, boot makers and repairs, Emmanuel Church, Gun Brewery and the Shakespeare Hotel – were all demolished in 1972 to make way for the new Northern Distributor Road. This present-day picture shows how the area has been completely transformed. The premises mentioned would have stood where this centre reservation is today.

Cheriton Road, looking across Guildhall Street into Shellons Street in May 1972. The Shakespeare Hotel seen here on the left was in business from 1847 to 1972 when it was demolished, along with all the houses the eye can see in Shellons Street, to make way for the new Northern Distributor Road.

This present-day picture shows a complete transformation of the area when compared to the earlier picture. The building on the right is at the junction of Guildhall Street, which has been completely cut through by the dual carriageway. In the middle distance can be seen Phoenix Court, the council flats in Clarence Street.

Looking along Guildhall Street from the junction of Shellons Street on the left and Cheriton Road on the right c.1905. On the right is the Shakespeare Hotel on the corner of Cheriton Road. It is interesting to note that by the lamp-post there is an upturned Tudor gun thought to have come from the Bayle Battery. It was from this that the Gun School, Gun Tavern and Gun Corner took their names.

This present-day picture was taken from the north-west side of Guildhall Street, formerly Shellons Lane. It shows the road cut in two by the dual carriageway. Some of the old street names have a historical basis: Shellons was the name of the field on the north-west side of Guildhall Street at the junction with Cheriton Road.

Looking down Shellons Street, formerly Griggs Lane, from the junction of Guildhall Street in May 1972. Demolition has begun prior to the construction of the Northern Distributor Road.

The new dual carriageway was completed in 1973 with a centre car park and bus lane. It was designed to keep the through traffic out of the town centre. The pedestrian crossing seen here is just below Guildhall Street, which this road divides.

Shellons Street looking down towards Grace Hill in 1979. This photograph was taken just before all the houses from the white house behind the lamp-post were demolished when the site became a temporary car park.

Shellons Street looking down towards Grace Hill in November 2001. Lidl's supermarket now sits on the site of the temporary car park, Lidl's opened on 3 October 1996. Shellons Street has retained its old name, extending up to Middleburg Square (formerly Bouverie Square). The north-west lane of the dual carriageway is called Foresters Way after the Foresters public house. The total cost of the Northern Distributor road was £1,000,000.

The Drill Hall in St Eanswythe's Terrace which ran from Shellons Street behind Guildhall Street. The Drill Hall was the home of the Territorial Army's 'D' Coy. 4th Bn – 'The Buffs'. It was demolished in April 1989 and the site was used as a temporary car park.

This road St Eanswyth's Way was named after St Eanswyth's Terrace and built as a service road for the pedestrianised Guildhall Street. The temporary car park site is now occupied by Lidl's supermarket and their car park, which opened on 3 October 1996.

Looking down Dover Road from Grace Hill in 1923. Among the businesses on the right-hand side are those of William Grinstead (confectioner), W.F. Bruce (furniture dealer), R. Todd (exchange and mart), G. Kettner (dealer in antiques and bookseller), S.H. Jones (tobacconist), J. Page (confectioner), T. Gosling (greengrocer) and Bridges & Co (carriers and furniture removers). Bridges & Co was the site of the Folkestone Dispensary, which was the forerunner of the Royal Victoria Hospital. On the left is the Wesleyan Church.

Looking down Dover Road today, one can see that all the shops on the right have disappeared; they were demolished in 1972. The Wesleyan Methodist Church has been replaced with Grace Court, a complex of sheltered flats, and it is interesting to note that Dover Road has been realigned.

Mr F.R. Radford, wheelwright of Park Lane, 1903-47. Park Lane ran from 12 Dover Road to 29 High Street (the gap by the Earl Grey Inn). In 1924 there were 16 businesses trading in Park Street. Park Lane and the surrounding area was originally an orchard owned by the Payer family hence the present name, Payer's Park.

The Council acquired the Payer's Park site, having accepted a purchase notice under the Town and Country Planning Act in 1965 to make a much-needed car park. In 1967 they acquired land on the frontage to Rendezvous Street to give improved access. In May 1987 the Council sold Payer's Park to Jimmy Godden for £170,000. Ever since then there have been numerous plans for the site, the last one in December 1999 to erect 135 one, two, and three-bedroom flats with 246 car parking spaces for public and private use.

Looking up Rendezvous Street about 1910. On the right are the offices of the Lydd Brewery, Finn Edwin & Sons, followed by Pickford Ltd (foreign and general carriers), the Baptist Church and Lewis, Hyland & Linom (general drapers, silk mercers milliners, costume, mantle makers and carpet salesmen). George Alexander Lewis founded his business in 1834. In 1867 the premises were demolished to allow for road widening and improvements to the street, at which time the present building was erected. By c.1870 the business had expanded and was called Lewis & Stapley. By 1896 the business had expanded again and was called Lewis, Hyland & Linom, and by c.1918 had taken on the familiar name of Lewis & Hyland.

Looking up Rendezvous Street today, the buildings occupied by the Lydd brewery office and Pickfords removals have been demolished. The Baptist Church has been transformed into a Wetherspoons public house and Lewis & Hyland's is now occupied by GHS Homemakers Store. The hoarding on the left marks the site of a fire, on 27 January 1990, at Mandolyn's fancy dress shop; the premises were subsequently demolished.

Looking along the top end of the Old High Street in 1973. In August 1796 the Commissioners of Paving changed the name of this end of the road from Bankersgate to Broad Street, which was later to become part of the High Street. Charles Yule, the house furnishers, were at these premises from 1953-72. The following buildings were occupied by Plummer Roddis, drapers, milliners and costumiers, from 1889 to 1972.

The Old High Street in November 2001. The building occupied by Yule's was demolished in May 1980 and a complex of shops and flats now occupy the site. The Plummer Roddis premises at 4 Old High Street – which, with its colonnade, was listed because of its architectural and historical interest – was finally demolished after being de-listed in 1984, with the proviso a colonnade is incorporated in the new building, as can be seen here in the complex of new shops and flats.

George Lane looking towards the High Street, pictured in 1973. The buildings on the left are part of the Plummer Roddis department store, while most of those on the right were occupied by Charles Yale, the house furnishers. At the end of George Lane in the Old High Street is Curtess's Shoe shop.

George Lane looking towards the High Street today. Plummer Roddis's department store was demolished in 1984 to make way for a complex of single-parent flats with shop units below. On the right the premises of Charles Yale were demolished in 1980 and a complex of flats with shop units below have been built on the site. The shop at the end of George Lane in the Old High Street, once a shoe shop, is now Big Top, a gift shop.

Looking up George Lane from the High Street in 1973. On the left of George Lane are the empty premises of Charles Yale followed by the Curzon cinema (which became the Cannon in 1974), formerly the Central. The building with the colonnade on the corner of George Lane and High Street was occupied by Plummer Roddis's department store until 1972.

The premises of Charles Yale were demolished in 1980 while the Cannon cinema was demolished in 1988, the sites of which are now occupied by a complex of flats with six shop units below, built by McCarthy and Stone. The premises of Plummer Roddis were demolished in 1984 to make way for this complex of one-parent flats with shop units below. Charlotte Emily's Victorian tearooms are under the colonnade.

This medieval house on the Bayle was erected no later than 1400. The house was altered in Tudor times with new fireplaces being inserted, and a small north-west wing added. Early in the 18th century it was converted into two tenements. This work was referred to in a deed of 1734. Last of all, the north-west wing was replaced by a larger one in weather boarding. There is no doubt that this building was one of the most important houses on the Bayle. It is most likely that in the Middle Ages, the Bayle formed the best residential part of Folkestone.

The *Folkestone Herald* moved to new offices and works on the site of the Old Harveian Institute, on the Bayle in December 1912. The medieval house, which stood next to the *Herald* offices, was demolished in 1916 and the site was used to extend the newspaper's offices and works. In November 1984 the newspaper moved to Westcliff House in Westcliff Terrace. The *Folkestone Herald's* former offices and print works in the Bayle were sold by auction in April 1985 and demolished in February 1989.

The site of the former *Folkestone Herald* offices and print works are now occupied by this complex of flats built by McCarthy & Stone, called Glendale. It consists of 48 one-bedroom flats for people over 60, a communal lounge, guest suite and laundry and secured private parking for residents.

Looking down Rendezvous Street in the early 1920s. By 1867, Rendezvous Street had been widened to 40ft and all the buildings were either reconstructed or new-fronted to designs of William Garstang, the architect. The pillar letterbox located at the entrance to George Lane is the site of the first letterbox erected in Folkestone in 1858. On the right are the businesses of Boots the Chemists, Stevenson (tobacconist), Plummer Roddis (drapers, silk, merchants, milliners, costumiers and complete house furnishers) and the Rose Hotel.

Looking down Rendezvous Street today. APR Estates Ltd, under the directorship of Anthony Pound, completely transformed the street, calling it the Lanterns and fitting Victorian shop fronts to their premises. This development was combined with Shepway Council's 'Focus' project, which consisted of repaving and new street lighting and fixtures. The shop on the corner of George Lane is now occupied by the Merchant Chandler, followed by Keith Graham's hairdressers, over which there are flats for single-parent families (formerly the site of Plummer Roddis, demolished in 1984) and next to that is a Victorian-style conservatory occupied by the Oriental Buffet. The Rose Hotel was demolished in 1928 to make way for Burton's new shop, which is now occupied by a bar called the Zoo.

Mr John Castle, the butcher, 4-6 Rendezvous Street. Mr Castle established his business between 1855 and 1858. The photograph was taken between October 1866 and February 1867. Long gone are the days when meat could be hung outside a shop. Today an environmental health inspector would most likely close the business down without warning.

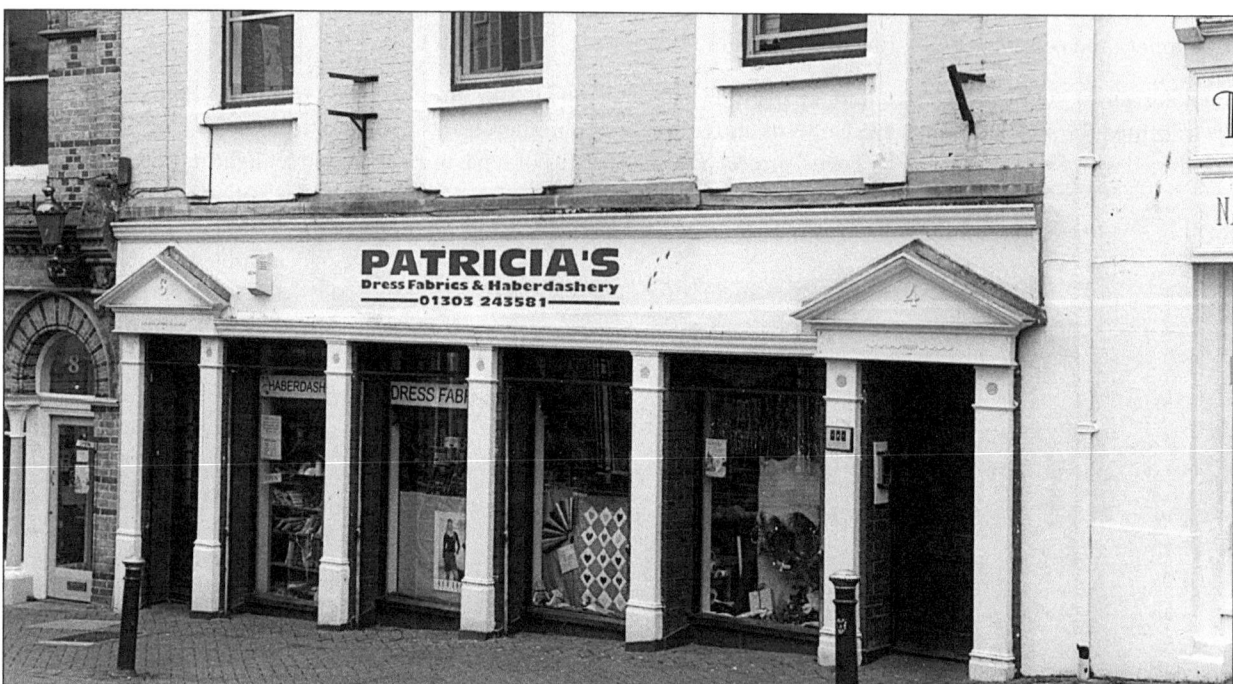

Mr Castle's butcher's shop was demolished during the road widening and redevelopment of Rendezvous Street, formerly Butcher Row, in 1867. The present-day premises were built on the site in 1867-8, and were designed by William Garstang. For many years the premises were occupied by Impacts clothing store but they closed in September 1997 and it is now occupied by Patricia's haberdashery.

Looking up Sandgate Road in 1910. On the left is the businesses of J.H. Bayly (fruiter and greengrocer), Thomas Boundy (fancy draper), John Price (jeweller and watchmaker), Upton Bros (fancy bazaar), and the East Kent Arms. On the right is the Queen's Hotel, Mark Bradwell (umbrella manufacturer), George Mount (florist), Uncle Tom's Cabin, Thomas E. Wing (tobacconist), Bodega (Queen's Hotel, its manager being Sidney T. Poore), T.G. Heron (grocer, provision, wine and spirit merchant) and the National Provincial Bank of England Ltd, the manager being Frank Scarborough.

Looking up Sandgate Road today. The street was pedestrianised in 1984. On the left is the business of Baguette & Run, and Marks & Spencer Ltd's departmental stores, followed by the East Kent Arms. On the right is Queen's House, the ground floor being occupied by Bonmarchè ladies clothing store, followed by the Card Fair Outlet, Quicksilver, Virgin Shop, Clinton Cards and Woolworths.

The Town Hall was built on the site of the Old Cistern House in 1860. It was designed by Joseph Messenger and built by the local contractor Mr John Edwards. At the basement level there was a covered market place, room for fire engines, six cells for prisoners, and the town sergeant's kitchen, beneath which there were spacious wine vaults. On the ground floor the front entrance, the vestibule and the principal staircase to the assembly room occupied the centre of the building facing Sandgate Road; to the right and left there were reading and justice rooms, a magistrates' room, and five rooms for the accommodation of the town sergeant, the police, and the rate collector. An assembly hall, a council chamber and a robing room occupied the first floor. The second floor contained the orchestra, commodious lumber rooms and the clock chamber. The front of the building is built with Portland stone in Italian style and is surmounted with a pediment containing an illuminated clock, the gift of the MP for the borough, Baron Meyer A. Rothschild. The inauguration took place on Wednesday 15 June 1861 followed by a vocal and instrumental concert under the direction of Mr W.B. Tolputt, organist of St Mary's Church. Mr Bowley, clerk of the works, tastefully decorated the hall with flags of all the nations being placed around the room and the Royal Standard over the principal entrance to the hall.

The Town Hall was put up for auction in 1986 and it was sold to the India Pru Company for £180,000. The India Pru spent £750,000 on restoring the listed building after which the ground floor was let in 1987 to Superdrug. The upper floor was let to the Silver Screen Cinema Company. The cinema opened on 20 April 1990 with the film *Hunt for Red October* (starring Sean Connery) and the Oscar-winning *Driving Miss Daisy*. The ground floor is now occupied by Waterstone's bookshop. Waterstone's was officially opened on Saturday 6 December 1997 by an actor called 'The Good Doctor', otherwise known as Tom Baker; he was signing copies of his autobiography *Who on Earth is Tom Baker?*

Liptons Ltd, the grocers, at 29 Sandgate Road. This was formerly part of the premises occupied by J.H. & J. Brooke the wine merchants, who opened a branch here in July 1864. Liptons took this business over from Vye & Sons Ltd in 1973. The sign in the right-hand window is advertising German Deacando Butter at 44p.

The grocery business of Liptons, a small supermarket chain, at 29 Sandgate Road closed in 1982 due to competition from the larger supermarkets. The shop has since been occupied by Thomas Cook, the travel agents.

The lower end of Sandgate Road, looking towards the Town Hall c.1866. Sandgate Road was anciently known as Cow Street. The lower end of the street became known as Sandgate Road in December 1822. The tall building on the right is the business of J.H. & J. Brooke, wine and spirit merchants who opened this branch in July 1864. Further down the road the protruding sign belongs to the East Kent Arms. It is interesting to note that most of the properties on the left-hand side are private dwellings with small front gardens, garden walls and railings.

The present-day view of the lower end of Sandgate Road – Folkestone's main shopping centre – looking towards Waterstone's bookshop. The road became a shopping precinct in 1984 and with its modern shop fronts has significantly transformed the street from the earlier photograph.

West Cliff Gardens at the junction of Sandgate Road. Number one West Cliff Gardens, on the corner of Sandgate Road, was a lodging house run by Miss McDermott. It was demolished to build 29 Sandgate Road (now 41) which was first occupied in 1895 by Temple, F. Wilson & Co, auctioneers, surveyors and house agents. The London City and Midland Bank board of directors decided to open a branch in Folkestone and on 29 September 1899 it was announced that suitable premises at 29 Sandgate Road had been found at a rental of £350 per annum. The bank opened on 18 May 1900. In 1922 the bank acquired the adjoining building (as seen here) to extend its premises.

West Cliff Gardens at the junction of Sandgate Road. In 1924 the new building designed by T.B. Whinney and built in Portland stone became the Midland Bank. The Midland amalgamated with the Hong Kong and Shanghai Banking Corporation in 1999. The official date when the sign was changed to HSBC was 27 July 1999.

Looking down Sandgate Road from the junction of Alexandra Gardens towards the Town Hall about 1918. On the corner of West Cliff Gardens can be seen the London City and Midland Bank (1900-23). On the left is the business of J. Weston & Son, photographers. Mr Weston established his business at 4 Eaton Place, Mill Lane (Dover Road) in 1865. He moved to 3 Guildhall Street in 1866 and in 1872 he moved to these premises where he remained until the business closed in 1922.

Looking down the shopping precinct in Sandgate Road from the junction of Alexandra Gardens towards Waterstone's bookshop in the old Town Hall. The shop occupied by J. Weston in the previous picture is now Evans, the ladies clothing store. On the right is the HSBC Bank, formerly the Midland Bank and the London City and Midland Bank.

Alexandra Gardens at the junction of Oxford Terrace, looking towards Bouverie Road East. The first shop from Oxford Terrace is occupied by G. Cox (the Empress Dog Parlour), followed by R. Quaife's hairdressing, and Barnardo's charity shop. This Victorian terrace was compulsory purchased by the Council and demolished in 1978. It is interesting to note that the one-way system is running in the opposite direction to that which it does today.

Looking along Alexandra Gardens from Oxford Terrace to Shellons Street (formerly Bouverie Road East). This land, which was used as a car park and weekly market, has been the subject of a number of planning applications since the early 1970s. Permission was given for a supermarket development in 1983, but the option was not taken up. On 2 April 1987 the land was sold by public auction to National Car Parks for £500,000. Today the left-hand side of the street is being demolished, along with the north-east side of Bouverie Square, to build a £35 million shopping centre over the whole area.

After the demolition of the Hotel Esplanade, 57 & 59 Sandgate Road, which was occupied by Seeboard, became unsafe. After a warning on 24 August 1974 that the building might collapse, 85 staff were evacuated. Seeboard moved to a mobile unit in Cheriton Place before moving to premises in Rendezvous Street on the corner of George Lane, previously occupied by Boots the Chemists who had moved to their new shop in Sandgate Road. Seeboard's Sandgate Road premises were demolished in October 1974.

W.H. Smith Ltd moved from 86 Sandgate Road to this new building at 57-59 Sandgate Road, which is on the site of the old Seeboard shop. Seeboard subsequently moved into 86 Sandgate Road previously occupied by W.H. Smith.

Frederick Bobby purchased 48 to 60 Sandgate Road, known as Albion Terrace, in March 1914 to build a new department store. World War One delayed the development so Messrs Bobby & Co generously placed at the disposal of Belgian refugees the seven houses. Three of them can be seen on the right of this photograph which shows local dignitaries entertaining the Belgian Consul by taking him for an outing to Canterbury Cathedral in 1915.

Albion Terrace at 48-60 Sandgate Road was demolished to build this department store for Bobby & Co Ltd, who moved into the premises from Rendezvous Street on Friday 6 March 1931. Numbers 62, 64 and 66 Sandgate Road, which since 1932 had been occupied by Lewis & Hyland (fashion specialists, ladies' outfitters, millinery and furnishers), were purchased by Bobby's in August 1935. The final advertisement for Bobby's appeared in the *Folkestone Herald* on Saturday 2 December 1972 before the firm was taken over by Debenhams.

Looking down Sandgate Road from the junction of Bouverie Place in 1937. The building on the corner of Bouverie Place had previously been occupied by Martin Walter (automobile engineers and coachbuilders) from 1923-31, and Lewis & Hyland (ladies outfitters) from 1932-5. The street is decorated for Folkestone's Floral Festival.

Looking down Sandgate Road from the junction of Bouverie Place in December 2001. The pedestrian precinct was built in 1984, from this junction down to the bottom of Sandgate Road, Rendezvous Street and along Guildhall Street. There were many mixed feelings among traders at the time; some thought it a good idea and some not. The trees planted among the street furniture have grown to such an extent, that they have blocked the view down the precinct.

Looking up Sandgate Road from West Terrace in the 1870s. Mr John William Stainer conducted his pharmaceutical chemist business from these premises, 59 Sandgate Road (corner of West Terrace), from 1867-70 to 1910. It is interesting to note that most of the buildings are still residential. The town's drift towards the west had not started!

Sandgate Road looking west from the junction of West Terrace in December 2001. While most of the Victorian buildings are still in place, the ground floors have all been put to commercial use. Phones 4u now occupies the shop on the corner of West Terrace. In January 1994 this new one-way system with single-file traffic, two sets of traffic lights and a narrowed road was introduced between West Terrace and Cheriton Place at a cost of £60,000.

Looking down Sandgate Road from Shakespeare Terrace *c*.1910. It is interesting to note that all the buildings on the right-hand side of Cheriton Place are residential. The top end of Sandgate Road, formerly known as Cow Street – part of which is seen here – appears as Sandgate Road between 1817 and 1822.

Sandgate Road looking down from the junction of Shakespeare Terrace in December 2001. All the walled gardens seen in the last picture have disappeared and the ground floors have been converted into shops. All due to the town's continual westward drift.

Martin Walter Ltd, 145 and 147 Sandgate Road, on the corner of Shakespeare Terrace. This branch opened in 1931 and closed on 21 May 1991. Maltby's Motor Works and Garage are on the other corner of Shakespeare Terrace, at 141 and 143 Sandgate Road. They were in business at these premises from 1923 to sometime between 1940-7, after which it was taken over by Caffyns Ltd, motor engineers.

145 and 147 Sandgate Road, which were occupied by Martin Walter Ltd, has been divided into shop units called The Shakespeare Centre. Caffyn's, who were at 141 and 143 Sandgate Road, closed in December 1986. The premises are now occupied by Blockbuster videos.

Bibliography

The Hythe Sandgate and Folkestone Guide W. Tiffen, 1816.

The New Hand-Book & Guide To The Town & Port of Folkestone William Tiffen, 1850.

Mackie, S.J. *Folkestone and its Neighbourhood* J. English, 1856.

Stock, H. *Stock's Illustrated Handbook of Folkestone* Hamilton, Adams & Co, London, 1862.

English's Folkestone, Sandgate & Boulogne Guide J. English, 1862.

Creed's Handbook to Folkestone C. Creed, 1869.

Felix *Rambles Around Folkestone* W.G. Glanfield, 1913.

Moncrieff, John *Folkestone Past & Present* F.J. Parsons, 1954.

Borough of Folkestone: The Council – its Services and Administration 1939-1968 by authority of the Council, March 1968.

Bishop, Dr C.H. *Folkestone: A Story of a Town* Headley Brothers, 1973.

Hart, Brian *Folkestone's Cliff Lifts* Millgate Publishing Company, 1985.

Whitney, Charles *Folkestone A Pictorial History* Phillimore, 1986.

Rooney, Eamonn and Alan Taylor, Charles Whitney *Folkestone in Old Photographs* Alan Sutton, 1990.

Humphreys, Roy *Target Folkestone* Meresborough Books, 1990.

Taylor, Alan F. and Eamonn D. Rooney *Folkestone in Old Photographs: A Second Selection* Alan Sutton, 1992.

Taylor, Alan F. *Britain in Old Photographs: Folkestone, A Third Selection* Alan Sutton, 1995.

Paine, J.M. and K.S. Paine *The History of the Leas Cliff Hall & Leas Shelter, Folkestone* Folkestone & District Local History Society.

Paine, J.M. and K.S. Paine *The History of the Wampach Hotel* Folkestone & District Local History Society.

Easdown, Martin and Linda Sage *Rain, Wreck & Ruin* Marlin Publications, 1997.

Taylor, Alan F. *Images of England: Folkestone* Tempus Publishing, 1998.

Easdown, Martin *Victoria's Golden Pier* Marlin Publications, 1998.

Paine, J.M. and K.S. Paine *The Story of Bobby & Co Ltd, 1906-1999* PDC.

Easdown, Martin and Eamonn Rooney *Tales From The Tap Room* Marlin Publications, 2000.

Folkestone Express.

Folkestone Gazette.

Folkestone Herald.

Pike's Folkestone, Hythe and Sandgate Directories Various editions.

Parsons' Directory and Year Book for Folkestone and District Various editions.

Kelly's Directories of Folkestone Various editions.